CHAPTER 1

INTRODUCTION

> War no longer exists. Confrontation, conflict and combat undoubtedly exist all around the world–most noticeably, but not only, in Iraq, Afghanistan, and the Democratic Republic of the Congo and the Palestinian Territories–and states still have armed forces which they use as a symbol of power. Nonetheless, war as cognitively known to most non-combatants, war as battle in a field between men and machinery, war as a massive deciding event in a dispute in international affairs: such war no longer exists.
>
> — Rupert Smith, *The Utility Of Force*

A Brave New World?

As the U.S. military prepares for a transition in Afghanistan, the Army is trying to remain relevant in a new environment when the American military structure is facing a strong pressure to reduce its budget, personnel, and activities around the world, and budget. Furthermore, the Budget Control Act of 2011 and the subsequent Sequestration have placed additional burden on the U.S. military to further reduce its force and budget while the U.S. is attempting to "pivot" to Asia and dealing with the persistent fundamentalist threats from the Middle East and Central Asia. During this tumultuous time, many are concerned how to best position and posture the U.S. military for future conflicts under a considerable budget constraint (Dempsey 2014). Moreover, there are also many discussions on American military's future role in the world, focusing on either a "Strategic Pivot to Asia" (Clinton 2011; DOD 2012) or a continuation in the "Era of Persistent Conflict" (Casey 2007). The creation of Regionally Aligned Forces (RAF) is demonstrating and signaling Army's attempt to align itself and posture its forces with the strategic guidance in the National Security Strategy (White House 2010) and the

Quadrennial Defense Review (DOD 2010; DOD 2014). Yet, there is an active debate within the Army as to what is the right approach for the future (Odierno 2012). This internal debate has become more important due to recent events in Syria, South Sudan, Ukraine, and Iraq in which wars amongst the people have continued to play a significant role in determining and shaping security issues around the world. Despite the Obama Administration's effort to minimize America's role as the world's policeman, the current environment and global community still rely heavily on the United States and its military as a superpower and hegemon in shaping global affairs (Obama 2014).

From these recent debates about the best way to use and employ military forces in the current geopolitical environment and in the future, one has to examine the recent events as a reference in order to understand both the successes and shortcomings of our recent past. Since the end of the Cold War, the U.S. Army has conducted more operations focusing on non-state actors. From the Operations Other Than War (OOTW) concept during the 1990s to the recent Contingency Operations, the U.S. military has devoted more focus and attention toward this non-linear and non-traditional form of military operations. Furthermore, many of these operations, such as Operation Restore Hope in Somalia and Operation Joint Endeavor in Bosnia, have demonstrated that the U.S. Army needs new concepts and doctrine in order to remain a relevant military force in the world.

Identity conflict is an idea that can found in concepts such as Hybrid Wars (Hoffman 2007), New Wars (Kaldor 2012), and War Amongst the People (Smith 2004). Professor Mary Kaldor from the London School of Economics coined the concept of "New Wars" in 1999 and Kaldor argues that the nature of conflict during the post-Cold War era has transitioned from state to state conflict to non-state actors waging violence

2

against civilian populations (2012). Using the Bosnia/Herzegovina conflict during the 1990s as a case study, Kaldor points out that the motivation of new wars is vastly different from the traditional Clausewitzian concept of war (Kaldor 2012, 32-58). German political scientist Herfried Münkler reiterated this point of divergent and put additional emphasis on how other aspects of warfare have also influenced the contemporary environment (2004).

Kaldor (2012) and Münkler (2004) are not alone in their arguments on the nature of conflict around the world after the collapse of the Soviet Union; other experts (Van Creveld 1991; Smith 2005; Hoffman 2007) have also rendered similar opinions. Martin van Creveld, an Israeli military historian, first expressed his thoughts on the changing nature of warfare in *The Transformation of War* (1991). General (Retired) Rupert Smith wrote *The Utility of Force* (2005) that examines the nature of modern warfare, differing from the traditional definition. From these academic discussions, it is vital to examine how the U.S. Army conducted its operations since the end of the Cold War, with special emphasis on operations that focused on non-state actors.

Research Question

The primary research question is to examine whether identity conflicts have shaped U.S. Army's doctrinal thinking about war and conflict since the end of the Cold War. The assertion here is that identity conflicts have already altered U.S. Army's operations since the end of the Cold War because many recent conflicts have changed from state to state confrontations to non-state actors waging conflicts against the civilian populations or central governments. Given this type of operational environment, the U.S. Army has already conducted several operations in response to identity conflicts. Through

3

doctrinal, budgetary, and organizational analysis, it is clear that identity conflicts have shaped how the Army perceives itself and its mandated mission.

In addition, secondary research questions are essential in order to facilitate the analysis and discussion in addressing and answering the primary research question. First, one has to define the term "identity conflict." It is important to address this question because a clear delineation is necessary in order to describe what constitutes an identity. After all, nationality, race, ethnicity, religion, geographic location, language, and many other factors can form and shape an identity. Thus, one has to be specific in defining the term "war," "conflict," and "identity" in order to support the primary research question without overburdening and inundating it with endless analysis. Furthermore, this chapter will provide a brief definition to the term "identity conflict" and the next chapter will operationalize the term with support from scholarly works.

Secondly, it is important to understand whether the U.S. Army has participated in any operation since the end of the Cold War involving an identity conflict between different groups. This question is pertinent because experience matters in shaping organizational level thinking. Furthermore, operational experience, especially in conflict zones, often dominates the direction of a military organization. This research project utilizes two case studies, Bosnia and Iraq, to illustrate U.S. Army's involvement in this type of conflict.

The third question is to address whether the U.S. Army has changed and modified its capstone doctrine as result of these operational experiences and lessons learned in places such as the Balkans and Iraq. Of course, one has to be cognizant that operational experience account for only one aspect of doctrinal change. Other areas such as national strategy and joint doctrines are also influential in the development of Army doctrine. Nonetheless, operational experience in places such as Bosnia and Iraq affects not only the U.S. Army but the entire U.S. government and other military services as well.

Assumptions

In constructing this thesis, several key assumptions are necessary in order to continue research. Furthermore, establishing these assumptions would enable others, in conducting similar research in the future, to understand how this research was conducted. Lastly, there are many unknowns out there. New data, reports, and untold personal stories could alter the research process.

The first key assumption is that all sources contain some sort of partiality. These sources can generally be trusted insofar as their methods and findings because this research employs factual-based findings and research results such as academic journals, major newspaper, government and reputable NGO reports. While it is entirely possible that some of the information might contain certain errors, these flaws should not distort the research process because this thesis conducts cross-referencing to ensure accuracy of all information provided.

The second assumption is that any information that has not been released, complied, or analyzed will not drastically change the outcome of this research project. Although any new information has the potential to alter the result of a research project, this project examines a current situation that has abundant information readily available. Many of the participants have already given their perspectives and shared their experiences in interviews, reports, or other written works. Thus, it is necessary to assume that any new information available in the future will not drastically alter the findings of this project.

Scope and Limitation

It is also crucial to outline the scope and limits of this research, providing an accurate self-assessment as to the range and possible shortfalls due to time and other constraints. First, this research's analysis focuses primarily on the U.S. Army. Some would argue that it is difficult to study American military operations during the post-Cold War era without analyzing the U.S. Marine Corps and its experience during this period. It is true that the Marines Corps has often conducted operations in support of non-traditional military operations such as Non-Combatant Evacuation Operations or Shows of Force. However, a key purpose here is to examine the Army's operations whether they have affected Army's perspective on war and conflict.

Secondly, the scope of this research focuses on the U.S. Army and its ability to adopt and modify as result of its operational experiences in Bosnia and Iraq. It is not an attempt to provide another perspective on the existing peace and conflict studies or offering new insight into why people choose violent means to settle disputes. Nonetheless, literature from conflict studies will enrich the discussion of this research. These academic ideas will contribute another perspective to the overall analysis, but this research has no intention to create a new theoretical approach to the existing body of knowledge on peace and conflict studies.

Thirdly, this research relies heavily on the existing material provided within the U.S. Army archives such as the U.S. Army Center for Army's Lessons Learned (CALL) to provide the bulk of data and information needed in the analytical portion of this research project. Additional sources, such as previously conducted interviews, also play an integral part in the analysis. One has to recognize that it is not possible to interview all key officials during this period and many of the existing interviews might not provide all the required material. Nonetheless, this research project utilizes other means such as newspaper reports, academic journals, and think tank reports to augment any shortcoming as result of a shortage in available primary sources.

In addition, this research has attempted to broaden the scope by incorporating scholarly works from those thinkers who are not generally associated with traditional security structures such as government agencies or government sponsored institutions. Works from Kaldor (2012) and Münkler (2004) are valuable in an attempt to bring a different perspective to examine the research question. By making an active attempt to avoid any research bias, this thesis applies critical thinking throughout the entire process to prevent partiality in its analysis.

Lastly, this research project has chosen to exclude materials that would prevent the publication of this research to all. Within the current environment, the inclusion of materials under certain government classification would result in limited publication only to those who have authorization. This runs contrary to the principles of academic research. It is a deliberate decision to exclude materials that would prevent full access to this research. In complimenting this shortfall, this research utilizes alternative means such as interviews or unclassified reports to ensure that the exclusion of classified materials will not undermine its quality.

Definition of Terms

One of the essential tasks in this chapter is to define important terms in order to ensure clarity and understanding. It is important to provide a framework and context in how these terms will be used. Furthermore, it will prevent others misconstruing and misusing these terms in other contexts or experiences. This section–through official documents, authoritative references, and scholarly works–will define war, conflict, identity, and the term identity conflict.

Looking at scholarly literatures, Clausewitz defines war as "not merely an act of policy but a true political instrument, a continuation of political intercourse, carried on with other means" (1976, 87). Clausewitz's quote has been a commonly used phrase and placed a special emphasis on the nature of war with politics. It adds another dimension and layer of complexity to the existing definition. More recently, Colin S. Gray repeated the same sentiment by stating that "war [is] to some degree, organized violence motivated by political considerations . . . is about the distribution of power" (2010). Besides Gray, many other experts and practitioners all have debated and exchanged their views, but without a definitive result, on the meaning and the nature of war.[1] Thus, the prevailing view is that war derives mostly between or amongst states, which has a strong political affiliation with the intention of distributing or re-distributing power. Yet, another interpretation of war, largely based on a modern understanding, describes it as "[involving] heterogeneous, organized, mutual enmity, and violence between armed

---

[1] In 2010, the U.S. Army War College hosted a strategic conference where experts such as Martin Van Creveld, Antulio Echevarria, Conrad Crane, Thomas Hammes, Andrew Bacevich, and Frank Hoffman gathered to discuss the current and the future nature of warfare; see Metz and Cuccia (2011) for the summarized version of the event.

groups, on more than a minor scale, carried out with political objectives, possessing social-political dynamics" (English 2013, 6). This particular description challenges the traditional thinking about war and thus offers alternative perspective and complexity into the term itself.

Conflict is defined as "an encounter with arms; a fight, battle" with the characteristic of "a prolonged struggle" (OED 1989). This definition contains the characteristic of a protracted event. Different from war, the *Oxford English Dictionary* (OED) definition suggests that conflict has a more prolonged nature. This important aspect is valuable to the analysis in the later section. Examining from scholarly works, conflict is also a term that many often used in association with other words in describing certain phenomenon, in the context of security related fields. For example, religious conflict, ethnic conflict, tribal conflict, and racial conflict are all commonly used terms in labeling some of most the contentious relationship and interaction between any group of people. Peter Wallensteen, in discussing conflict resolution, defines conflict as "a social situation in which a minimum of two actors (parties) strive to acquire at the same moment in time an available set of scarce resources" (2002, 16). Also, Rangelov and Kaldor examined a few sources–to include the Uppsala Conflict Data Program, a prominent source used by many influential reports in the security studies–and discovered that conflict is very much a contested term that does not have a specific meaning (2012, 195). In the context of this thesis, conflict involves a protracted event or situation in which multiple parties are in competition, using violent and destructive means, over limited or finite resources.

Identity is another term that requires a specific definition. Identity defines as "the sameness of a person or thing at all times or in all circumstances; the condition of being a single individual; the fact that a person or thing is itself and not something else" (OED 1989). In short, it is about recognizing similarities that can be formed through religion, race, ethnicity, nationality, or tribe. At the same time, it is also about grouping one section together in contrast against all others, separating one from the others through partially formed and arbitrary selection, which contains a random and bias judgment favoring a particular sameness over all others.

Siniša Malešević wrote about "identity as ideology" and provided an in-depth discussion from the perspective of nationalism and ethnicity (2006). Malešević argues that, from a social science view, identity "covers too much ground to be analytically useful" and is "ill-suited" to explain societal changes in last few decades (2006, 36-7). This argument largely echoes with the explanation provided in the OED. In addition to Malešević, other scholars have also provided additional perspective to the meaning of identity (Chandra 2006). In short, identity has become an "essentially contested concept."[2] Examining from this point of view, identity as a word has to be augmented by other words in order to provide an operationalized meaning in an analytical setting. Thus, one can conclude that identity is a complex concept and requires a thoughtful application in order to be a useful in the analytical section.

---

[2] W. B. Gallie coined the phrase in 1956. In his discussion, Gallie tried to examine "organized and semi-organized human activities: in academic terms . . . see that there is no one clearly definable general use of any of them" (1956, 168). This phrase has been used in areas such as security studies to examine the complexity of a subject (Mathews 1989; Baldwin 1997).

Within the context of this research project, identity conflict is defined as any group, using the method of self and others, to create a divide between or amongst different groups–by highlighting and exacerbating nationality, ethnic, racial, or religious difference–through the use of violence in achieving its intended goal or objective. This kind of violence can range from political protests to the extreme methods such as forced migration, government sanctioned atrocity, and genocide. Based on the discussion of war and conflict, identity conflict can operate on a continuum spectrum from a high level violence in case of an interstate war to a lower level of violence such as ethnic or sectarian conflict. This spectrum also spans from interstate, intrastate to intercommunal type of violence. Thus, it adds a layer of complexity that has confounded many people to create a viable solution to deal with such an issue. Also, identity conflict can be a prolonged process and has the possibility of transforming into a conventional war. Through this definition, the literature review chapter will provide a more detail theoretical argument about how this concept has evolved through time.

Point of Departure: Clausewitz, His Disciples, and FM 100-5

There is a fundamental idea that needs to be covered in this chapter. More specifically, it is the traditional perspective represented by Carl von Clausewitz and his writing *On War*, a classic work that includes an overly-quoted phrase of "war as an extenuation of politics by other means" (1976, 87). More recently, many modern military thinkers as such Antulio Echevarria, Hew Strachan, and others are still putting forth relevant and critical discussions on the impact of Clausewitz's idea in the contemporary setting. In the end, these ideas have largely manifested in the first post-Cold War manual, the 1993 version of FM 100-5, *Operations*.

The Grandmaster: Carl von Clausewitz

Clausewitz and his seminal work, *On War*, are a part of traditional military and strategic thinking, serving as an influential guide on war and strategy. Besides "war is merely the continuation of policy by other means" (Clausewitz, 1976, 87), one of central concepts in *On War* is that war as "more than a true chameleon that slightly adapts its characteristics to the given case" (1976, 89). This argument provides a foundation and understanding of war by emphasizing the adaptive characteristic of a war. From it, concepts such as the paradoxical trinity, friction, chance, and uncertainty are all important elements to the understanding of Clausewitz's meaning of war. Firstly, the paradoxical trinity consists of "primordial violence, hatred and enmity" which can be related to people, military and the government (Clausewitz 1976, 89). Many have understood the paradoxical trinity as a description of the traditional modern state concept with each nation-state interacting with military and people because Clausewitz was writing in the context of modern European states during the Napoleonic era.

In addition to the paradoxical trinity, friction, chance, and uncertainty are also important elements that one needs to understand. Clausewitz first explains the concept of friction as "the force that makes the apparently easy so difficult" (1976, 121). Understanding friction and its relationship with war, Clausewitz has chosen to emphasize the uncertainty in waging any type of military operation by mentioning that "the military machine is basically very simple . . . but we should bear in mind that none of its components is of one piece . . . every one of whom retains his potential of friction" (1976, 119). In short, these passages illustrate the importance of complexity and its influence in military thinking. Thus, friction, chance, and uncertainty are still important and relevant in understanding the current complex dynamics.

Clausewitz's Disciples

Many modern thinkers have tried to connect Clausewitz's idea to the contemporary environment (Howard 2002; Strachan 2007; Strachan 2008; Strachan 2011; Echevarria 2005; Echevarria 2007; Dasse 2007; Heuser 2007; Simpson 2012). For example, Hew Strachan has chosen to emphasize Clausewitz and his dialectics (2007). Within Clausewitz's work, Strachan focuses that "the existential nature of war," which derives from Clausewitz's 1812 manifesto and it represents an important element that disputes Kaldor's criticism of the "Old Wars" (2007, 37). Fundamentally, Strachan makes the point that Clausewitz is still important in today's world and no one should overlook these concepts as irrelevant or outdated. Like Strachan, Antulio Echevarria also tries to connect Clausewitzian ideas to the contemporary setting (2007). After challenging the utility of Hammes's Fourth Generation Warfare argument (see Echevarria 2005), Echevarria took on the task of analyzing Clausewitz's work within the contemporary setting in *Clausewitz and Contemporary War* (2007). From this work, Echevarria was aiming to achieve two goals: understand the purpose of *On War* and its methodology (Echevarria 2007, 2) and transform that knowledge as a basis in understanding theory or war, relationship between war and politics, and finally strategy (2007, 19). Through this analysis, Echevarria represents a position that Clausewitz can be useful and applicable in the contemporary environment. These scholars have consistently argued that Clausewitzian ideas are relevant even after the Cold War because his ideas represent timeless military and strategic principles.

13

Initial Post-Cold War Concept:
The 1993 version of FM 100-5

In the aftermath of the Cold War, the 1993 version of FM 100-5 made a significant revision from the existing "Air-Land" Battle Doctrine (US Army 1986) toward a more a broad spectrum discussion that includes the Range of Military Operations, separating the strategic environment into war, conflict, and peacetime (US Army 1993, 2-1). More specifically, the manual created two distinct categories for military operations: War and Operations Other Than War (OOTW). Through the description of war, conflict, and peacetime in Figure 1, it is clear that the Army was still focusing on the high intensity level of war. Although FM 100-5 attempted to address the issue of OOTW in a new and changing environment, the manual placed "war preparation as Army's top priority . . . the overall emphasis remained war, for the chapter on OOTW consisted of but nine of the manual's 173 pages" (Kretchik 2011, 227). Furthermore, OOTW contains operations ranging from strikes and raids to peacekeeping. With such a diverse field and little space devoted in the actual discussion, the 1993 version of FM 100-5 did not adequately address the actual changes in the post-Cold War environment. This lack of clarity would become a problem later. An evolution of Army's capstone doctrine would occur as result of many inadequacies in the 1993 version of FM 100-5.

STATES OF THE ENVIRONMENT	GOAL	MILITARY OPERATIONS	EXAMPLES
WAR	Fight and Win	WAR	• Large-scale combat operations . . . • Attack • Defend
CONFLICT	Deter War and Resolve Conflict	OTHER THAN WAR	• Strikes and raids • Peace enforcement • Support to insurgency • Antiterrorism • Peacekeeping • NEO
PEACETIME	Promote Peace	OTHER THAN WAR	• Counterdrug • Disaster relief • Civil support • Peace building • Nation assistance

The states of peacetime, conflict, and war could all exist at once in the theater commander's strategic environment. He can respond to requirements with a wide range of military operations. Noncombat operations might occur during war, just as some operations other than war might require combat.

Figure 1.   FM 100-5 Range of Military Operations

Source: Department of the Army, Field Manual (FM) 100-5, *Operations* (Washington, DC: Government Printing Office, 1993), 2-1.

The 1993 version of FM 100-5 attempted to address the post-Cold War environment by discussing OOTW with all its variations. Theoretically, the 1993 version of FM 100-5 is a document that continues to address many of the Clausewitz concepts in its understanding of the post-Cold War world. In addition to its continual emphasis on war, a primarily state on state type of major conflict, the 1993 version of FM 100-5 also contained themes such as Principles of War and Tenets of Army Operations while incorporating friction, chance, and uncertainty as some of the key elements. In short, this document maintained many of the Clausewitzian ideas. Continuing to focus on the traditional form of warfare as its primary mission, the 1993 FM 100-5 did not accurately foresee and predict the kind of military mission the U.S. Army would involve itself in the new operational environment. The manual mentions "forces are likely to encounter conditions of greater ambiguity and uncertainty" but it also stresses that "the American people expect decisive victory [and] prefer quick resolution of conflicts" (US Army

15

1993, 1-1-3). Using the will and wishes of American people as a pretext, the 1993 FM 100-5 precluded to see a long and extended military operation as a possibility. Moreover, it offers no discussion on human domain as a factor for either war or conflict. The 1993 version of FM 100-5, the first post-Cold War capstone doctrine, would face various challenges and criticism during operations in Haiti, Bosnia, and Kosovo.

Thesis Outline

A roadmap is important to serve as a guide for the remainder of this thesis. Chapter 2 will focus on various literatures with emphasis on war and conflict. The literature review section will focus on the "New Wars" theory as the principle theoretical framework for the identity conflict thesis. More specifically, Mary Kaldor (2012), Herfried Münkler (2004), and Rupert Smith (2005) will provide the main framework through the "New Wars" theory and concepts such as "War Amongst the People." In addition, the literature review will also examine military doctrinal development and framework as a reference in understanding the evolution of various doctrinal changes. The purpose of literature review is to identify important scholarly arguments and discussion on the characters of war and conflict in the modern world. More importantly, the literature review will also provide a valuable theoretical foundation for the remainder of this research project.

Following the literature review, the methodology section will discuss the basic research method that will demonstrate the validity of the overall argument. In doing this research, qualitative method will be the principle research method. More specifically, two case studies with four evaluation criteria will serve as the basis for the analytical portion of this thesis.

16

The analytical section addresses the primary and some of the key secondary research questions by looking at Bosnia and Iraq. By using the evaluation criteria established in the methodology chapter, the analytical section focuses on examining materials provided in each case study to further analyze and decipher whether the U.S. Army has adequately addressed the issue of identity conflict as an important character of contemporary warfare and armed conflict. In addition, the analytical section concentrates on the evaluation criteria provided as a tool to answer the primary research question. More specifically, this research looks closely at the development of Army's capstone doctrine, FM 3-0, as a way to understand and analyze whether the Army has recognized identity conflict as an important character of war in contemporary armed conflict.

Summary

As stated earlier in this chapter, the purpose of this research project is to question whether the "identity conflict" concept has affected the U.S. Army doctrine, using Bosnia and Iraq as two case studies. Rather than repeating various existing literature and official documents complied as part of Army's lessons learned, this research project uses theoretical concepts merged from various scholarly works in order to thoroughly examine the effect of the operations in the Balkans has on today's Army. This chapter has identified and established many of the key foundations that are necessary for the future chapters. In addition to stating the purpose of this project, this chapter has also put forth the research questions, assumptions, terms, limitations, and scope of this thesis. Lastly, this research has provided an outline to serve as a guide in the reading of this thesis. The next chapter will examine key concepts and their criticism, providing the theoretical foundation for this project.

CHAPTER 2

LITERATURE REVIEW

This purpose of this chapter is to provide an overview of key scholarly arguments on the characters of war and conflict since the end of the Cold War. Most of these arguments are questioning whether warfare has changed from the state on state focus toward non-state actors playing a more critical and central role. More importantly, the collapse of the Soviet Union and Warsaw Pact's disintegration had also ushered in a new era in which the constant competition between the United States and the Soviet Union ceased. With the end of bipolarity paradigm between two superpowers, many have wondered and argued about the future (Fukuyama 1992; Layne 1993; Huntington, 1993). Whether it was Samuel Huntington's *Clash of Civilization* or Francis Fukuyama's *The End of History*, wars and conflicts were still happening during the post-Cold War era and many of these conflicts were more destructive than those wars during the Cold War period. Yet, the traditional political theorists could not adequately explain the recent wars and conflicts.

Although political theorists like Huntington and Fukuyama provided an overarching view of the global landscape about the post-Cold War world, these concepts could not sufficiently explain the complexity of war or armed conflict. After all, there were many wars and conflicts that had occurred which had nothing to do with either clashing of culture values or ideology. For example, the Great African Wars–largely occurred as result of the Rwanda conflict following the genocide in 1994–could not be sufficiently explained through either Huntington or Fukuyama's analysis. In addition, many of these theories focus on the big ideas such as realism, liberalism, constructivism, and critical theory, with each theory trying to provide its own explanation about the nature of the post-Cold War era without providing any specificity in understanding the nature of conflict.[3] While it is important to recognize the contribution of each international relations theory in the larger framework, these theoretical concepts are insufficient, by themselves, in explaining contemporary wars and conflicts. Therefore, one has to focus on literatures that devote a greater attention and importance toward the analysis of war and conflict.

This chapter begins with a discussion on the "New Wars" theory (Kaldor 2012; Münkler 2005) and "War Amongst the People" (Smith 2005), with each providing a perspective on the concept of "identity conflict." Through a thorough discussion, one can better understand how this "Changing Character of War" (Strachan and Scheipers 2013, 1) has influenced the current environment and why identity conflict has become a recurring theme in the contemporary operational environment.

This chapter also examines the concept of military doctrine and its evolution by looking at some of the theoretical concepts and actual evolution through time as a way to understand various adaptations and evolutions. Aaron Jackson's writing (2013) and Chris Paparone (2008) serve as an important foundation to this discussion. Also, this chapter relies on official military doctrines from the U.S. and UK as a key reference to how doctrine is defined. Furthermore, Walter Kretchik (2011) and Andrew Birtle (2006; 2011) provide meaningful contributions to the understanding of doctrine.

---

[3] This paper will not attempt to provide a detailed discussion on each theory due to the complexity of each argument and associated variations such as neo-realism or neo-liberalism. For a general discussion and analysis on the impact and contribution of each theory, see Buzan and Hansen (2009) and Snyder (2004).

In the end, this section synthesizes both perspectives and capture critical points that would enable a better understanding in "identity conflict" during the analytical section. Although this research will not attempt to combine or merge two diverging views, a theoretical feat that would be quite difficult to accomplish, it is important to draw out the similarities between these two opposing sides and identify the shortcomings of each argument in order to provide a more thorough and comprehensive understanding.

The "New Wars" Theory: Kaldor, Münkler, and Smith

Different from the traditional way of thinking, there are numerous writings analyzing and discussing the characteristics of post-Cold War conflicts (see Van Creveld, 1991; Holsti, 1996; Hammes, 2006; Hoffman, 2007). The "New Wars" theory seems to attract most of the attention and controversy. Combined with Rupert Smith's writing in *The Utility of Force* (2005), the "New Wars" theory has become a key and dominant perspective in analyzing the post-Cold War environment.

Kaldor's "New Wars" Theory

Mary Kaldor's "New Wars" theory, formulated during the 1990s, is one of the key concepts that try to facilitate the discussion and understanding of the post-Cold War environment. Through an analysis on the Bosnia/Herzegovina conflict, Kaldor constructed the "New Wars" theory and challenged the existing presumptions about the contemporary characters of war and conflict (2012). Framing the argument within the context of globalization, Kaldor identified three distinct characteristics of the "New Wars" theory that are different from the "Old Wars" (2012, chapter 1). First, "New Wars" have different goals than from the previous state on state conflicts (2012, 7).

20

Kaldor argues that, "the political goals of the new wars are about the claim to power on the basis of seemingly traditional identities–nations, tribe, religion . . . the politics of particularistic identities cannot be understood in traditional term" (2012, 71). In short, this argument points out that the goals, some would call objectives or end states, are different from the state on state conflicts. From this perspective, one cannot accurately translate the goals of the state on state conflict to the post-Cold War environment. In addition, Kaldor identified a key difference, identity, which differs from past conflicts. Identity, according to Kaldor, is focusing on ethnic, tribe, racial or religious recognition (2012, 79). The intent is to concentrate on the identity politics of the post-Cold War era rather than focusing on identity as a term commonly used colloquially because the common usage of conflict, which could have many different definitions depending on the subject, does not provide a meaningful context to the larger framework of the conflicts occurred amongst different people.

The mode of warfare is another key area. Instead of capturing territory by military means, a defining character in traditional warfare, territory is "capture through political control of the population rather than through military advance [and] the aim is to control the population by getting rid of everyone of a different identity" (Kaldor 2012, 9). In short, this is about removing the "others" from ones territory for the pursuit of identity, whatever the form it might be. It is also in this kind of pursuit that one would see massive refugees or internal displaced people as another component in the "New Wars" theory (Kaldor 2012, 9). Referencing again to the concept of identity, the mode of warfare centers around how one group uses methods such as mass killing, forced resettlement, or economic intimidation to achieve the goal of removing those with a different identity.

21

Rather than targeting government offices or officials as in the case of traditional insurgency, civilians have become the target and victim in the "New Wars" (Kaldor 2012, 55). Furthermore, the perpetrator of these violent acts can include paramilitary groups, local warlords, criminal gangs, mercenary groups and as well as breakaway regular armies (Kaldor 2012, 9-10). Using Bosnia as a case study, Kaldor describes both the Serbian and Croatian paramilitary groups and gangs systematically committed atrocities or other forms of intimidation against Bosnian Muslims in order to create an autonomous region of the same ethnicity (2012, 45-54). To successfully plan and execute an ethnic cleansing, it would require a sufficient and steady financial base to sustain this type of operation.

War economy is the third and last important feature in Kaldor's "New Wars" theory (2012, 10). In the post-Cold War setting, war economy means more than just the ability to finance and gather resources to support a war through taxation or borrowing. Nation states have largely used the selling of treasury notes or bonds as a traditional apparatus to finance wars and smaller scale armed conflicts. Within the context of "New Wars," local or non-state actors have resorted to methods such as plunder, drug-trafficking, hostage-taking, black market, or taxing humanitarian assistance to finance their activities (Kaldor 2012, 10). Although many scholarly works have written quite extensively about these methods of financing non-traditional conflicts (Collier and Hoeffler 1998; Collier and Hoeffler 2004; Fearon 2005; Ross 2004), Kaldor specifically linked this type of financing method as a characteristic of "New Wars" in the contemporary setting (2012, chapter 5). In addition, Kaldor also examines and explains how remittances from abroad, direct assistance from the diaspora community, foreign assistance and humanitarian assistance have also contributed to non-state actors' ability finance themselves (2012, 109-111). Once again, this type of activities puts emphasis on support one particular group and thus reaffirming the identity issue that is so crucial in understanding the contemporary setting of the "New Wars" theory.

Despite her best attempt to characterize a changing environment, there are several important critiques to Kaldor's argument and these critics challenge the argument that "new wars" are a phenomenon occurring only after the end of the Cold War (Newman 2004; Berdal 2004; Schuurman 2010; Echevarria 2007). First, Newman argues that the "New Wars" concept lacks a proper historical perspective (2004). Newman emphasizes that "a number of historical forces and processes have had an impact on the nature and impact of war. Decolonization and state-building, proxy Cold War conflicts . . . have all arguably had an impact . . . it is problematic to asset a *general* [sic] departure/change from the past" (2004, 180). In short, most contemporary wars and armed conflicts have a long historical root. In addition to Newman criticism, Mats Berdal also challenges the validity of "New Wars" theory (2003). Berdal reiterates some of Newman's criticism of Kaldor's argument while focusing on its lack of precision (2003, 481). In short, Kaldor (2012) has encountered a steady stream of criticism. After examining critiques from Berdal (2003) and Newman (2004), it is clear that Kaldor's argument (2012) still needs to be complimented by other ideas to remain as a relevant approach in understanding the post-Cold War environment.

Herfried Münkler's Complimentary Argument

Also using the title of "New Wars," German political scientist Herfried Münkler (2004) constructed a similar argument that compliments much of Kaldor's thesis.

Münkler echoes some of Kaldor's emphasis on the suffering of civilian population and the privatization of armed conflict throughout the world (2004, 14-22). However, Münkler made several important and critical points on how he defined the "New Wars" theory (2004). First, Münkler concentrated on contemporary conflicts as "state-disintegrating wars" (2004, 8) and conflicts will persist much longer amongst societies (2004, 11). Although the concept of state-disintegration is not a unique or new argument (Posen 1993; Lake and Rothchild 1996), Münkler tries to link this kind of state-disintegration in the post-Cold War context with longer term and persistent conflict amongst different societies (2004, 8-13). Münkler (2004) reinforces Kaldor's central concept of identity conflicts in his argument about the long-term struggle, through state-disintegrating wars, amongst different societies. Furthermore, Münkler (2004) adds another component to the "New Wars" theory in which an identity based conflict or struggle will be a prolonged process.

Secondly, Münkler chose to use an important historical reference, the Thirty Years War, as an analytical framework for his work (2004, 42-50). By comparing the "New Wars" with the Thirty Years War, Münkler identified that "men under arms increasingly go over to using war as a means to personal enrichment and guns as an instrument for acting out of fantasies of omnipotence and sadism" as a striking similarity between the two war (2004, 44). In short, this approach enables Münkler to avoid and escape from those critiques (see Neumann 2004) that challenged Kaldor's argument (2012) as failing to understand history and approaching the "New Wars" theory merely from an ahistorical perspective.

Within the context of this thesis, Münkler (2004) serves as a complimentary volume to Kaldor's thesis (2012). Having the benefit of writing after Kaldor, Münkler (2004) was able to provide some of other details lacking in Kaldor's original concept (2012). However, there is another important literature that will further strengthen the concept of "New Wars" theory and identity conflicts.

Rupert Smith's War Amongst the People

General Sir Rupert Smith, a retired British Army officer with experience in both conventional and unconventional military operations, has put forth a practitioner's perspective that highlights Kaldor and Münkler's "New Wars" theory while trying to operationalize the concept. Analyzing and reflecting on the characteristics of war and conflict in the post-Cold War era, Smith coined the phrase of "War Amongst the People', characterizing the contemporary environment in a different outlook from the traditional paradigm of "interstate industrial war (2005, 18). Echoing many of the arguments made from Kaldor and Münkler, Smith identifies six trends that reflect the reality of the new form of war (2005, 20). Of the six trends that best characterizes Smith's "War Amongst the People" concept (2005), several trends are related to Kaldor and Münkler's "New Wars" theory. For example, Smith describes that the ends have changed from "hard absolute objectives of interstate industrial war to more malleable objectives to do with the individual and societies that are not states" (2005, 19). This trend directly relates to a characteristic of the "New Wars" theory in that goals and objectives have no longer as the same as before. There is a consensus and sentiment that today's environment is vastly different from yesterday's conventional or industrial wars. Fundamentally, Smith has a very similar outlook about the post-Cold War environment as Kaldor (2012) and Münkler (2004).

In addition to the previous point, Smith also emphasizes that conflicts tend to be timeless (2005, 19). This point reflects Münkler's argument (2004) that a conflict tends to last longer than a war. Both seem to reach the point that a definitive solution in resolving today's conflict might take "years or decades" (Smith 2005, 19). Secondly, Smith stresses the element of non-state actors in today's world in that "we tend to conduct our conflicts and confrontations . . . against some party or parties that are not states." (2005, 19-20). Once again, Smith points out one of the key elements of the "New Wars" theory, the rise of non-state actors in the post-Cold War environment, as a major trend in his assessment that "War Amongst the People" will be likely to continue to for the foreseeable future (2005, 415). In short, Smith made an argument from military practitioner's perspective based on recent experiences that conflict over identity, characterized as "War Amongst the People," will persist in the current state and this "must become a central part of our way ahead" (2005, 374).

The Evolution of Military Doctrine

Doctrine is invaluable and a necessity for any military organization. After all, the purpose of a doctrine is to provide "a common philosophy, language, purpose, and unity of effort for the employment of forces" (Ancker and Sculley 2013, 38). Furthermore, doctrine offers, "a distillation of experience, furnishing a guide to methods that have generally worked in the past and which are thought to be of some enduring utility" (Birtle 1998, 5). Also, Walter Kretchik argues that there is a peculiar relationship between informal practices and formal doctrine that one has to understand in order to grasp how

26

the U.S. Army has operated throughout history (2011, 5). In all, these discussions all concur with the concept that doctrine provides a common understanding for a group of people that has some enduring utility. At the same time, Kretchik (2011) argues that one has to consider the difference between a "formal doctrine" and "informal practices" in understanding the evolution of doctrinal development.

Similar to various scholarly discussions on the purpose of a doctrine, official perspectives display a very similar view. From the British military, doctrine is "an approved set of principles and methods, intended to provide large military organizations with a common outlook and a uniform basis for action" (UK Army 2011, 1-1). According the latest U.S. Army doctrine, doctrine defined as "fundamental principles, with supporting tactics, techniques, procedures, and terms and symbols, used for the conduct of operations and which the operating force, and elements of the institutional Army that directly support operations, guide their actions in support national objectives" (US Army 2014, 1-2). Although the American definition offers a more expansive definition than the British version, these official definitions all incorporate many of the same elements such as common principles for the purpose of organizational unity. In short, there is a consensus and understanding on the purpose of doctrine and its utility to a military organization.

Looking at it closely, military doctrine can be further broken into several schools and each has its purpose and significance. Aaron Jackson argues, based on his analysis on military doctrinal ontology, there are four schools of military doctrine: technical manual, tactical manual, operational manual, and military strategic manual (2013, 3). Each school has its importance and relevance to a military organization at a different place and time in history. For example, Jackson's study argues the technical manual has no relationship with military's ontology while the military strategic manual tries to "examine a broad range of ontological questions and pose answers to them" (2013, 11). In other words, those technical manuals focus only the mechanical aspects such as how to load and fire a rifle have little to no relevance in answering or framing the larger strategic question. On the other hand, military strategic doctrines "tend to be philosophical in nature, establishing fundamental principles or a core conceptual framework that is intended to describe, categorize, and justify military activities" (Jackson 2013, 29). Through time, military doctrine has largely evolved from the technical manuals to mostly operational manuals in the 1990s (Jackson 2013, 28). The end of Cold War and the uncertainty following this period triggered a move by many military institutions to transition from operational manuals to strategic manuals (Jackson 2013, 28-31). As a result, there is a closer link between a capstone manual and national security strategy.

Another perspective to understand military manual is Chris Paparone's analysis on the dichotomy between positivism and postpositivism (2008).[4] From Paparone's analysis, there are four categories to evaluate a capstone doctrine: Highly Positivist, Moderately Positivist, Moderately Postpositivst, and Highly Postpositivst (2008). Highly Positivist doctrine defines as "codification of knowledge with an emphasis on procedure learning" represented by the 1976 version of FM 100-5, while Moderately Positivist differs in its emphasis on "process rather than preset solutions and requires military staff with specialized training" (Paparone 2008). On the other end of spectrum, Highly

---

[4] It is important to point out that Paparone's concept of postpositivism differs from the traditional concept of postpositivism which is a critique of the traditional scientific inquiry method (see Popper 1959; Kuhn 1962).

Postpositivist doctrine defines as "experiential, macro-philosophy" and Moderately Postpositivist doctrine defines as "narrative oriented with a multidisciplinary studies background" (Paparone 2008). Through a more philosophical distillation, Paparone (2008) constructed these four types to both categorize and characterize the feature of each military doctrine. In short, both Jackson (2013) and Paparone (2008) have tried to offer a theoretical argument in understanding military doctrines.

Looking at some of the practical examples, Walter Kretchik and Andrew Birtle have both attempted to synthesize the evolution of U.S. Army doctrine with one focusing primarily on the development of capstone document (Kretchik 2011) and the other focusing on the counterinsurgency operations (Birtle 1998; Birtle 2006). In *U.S. Army Doctrine: From the American Revolution to the War on Terror*, Walter Kretchik provided an in-depth account, from a historical perspective, that examines the evolution of Army doctrine, focusing primarily on the capstone manual (2011). Furthermore, Kretchik gave a lot of credit to Clausewitz and Jomini in that they have "shaped the perceptions and approaches of U.S. Army leaders toward armed conflict" (2011, 1). Kretchik's book covers the development of Army's capstone doctrine from the American Revolution to War on Terror and provides an in-depth analysis on various discussions within the Army that led to the publication of various capstone doctrines (2011). Andrew Birtle (1998; 2006) also provides a similar discussion and historical analysis on the development of counterinsurgency manual within the U.S. Army from 1860 to 1976. Both of these authors and their works reflect a more practical analysis that focuses on the actual doctrine itself rather than theoretical arguments.

Summary: Synthesizing Ideas

This chapter has put together a collection of ideas on the characters of war and conflict since the end of Cold War. One has to evaluate both the strengths and shortcomings of each argument in order to formulate a consistent and coherent argument while capturing the key elements needed in order to continue this research process. As a way to define identity conflict, it is important to understand the key elements from each. Kaldor's "New Wars" theory (2012) started as an attempt to construct a framework in understanding the environment after the end of the Cold War. Three core ideas from Kaldor's "New Wars" theory are alternative goals, a different mode of warfare, and a new method to finance (2012). At the same time, Münkler focuses on the duration of conflict and state-disintegrating nature as his main emphasis of "New Wars" theory (2004). Lastly, Smith argues that "War Amongst the People" as a key attribute in the contemporary environment (2005). In short, these three authors and their ideas construct the philosophical basis for the identity conflict argument.

Literature review has also examined doctrinal development and its many variations. Jackson (2013) and Paparone (2008) provided key theoretical frameworks while Kretchik (2011), Birtle (1998), and Birtle (2006) offered actual historical examples through their analyses on U.S. Army's capstone and counterinsurgency doctrine. Each material provides an important perspective in framing the context for the actual discussion later in the analytical section.

CHAPTER 3

RESEARCH METHODOLOGY

The purpose of this research is to examine whether the U.S. Army, in its capstone doctrine, has accepted the identity conflict thesis as an important characteristic in understanding the contemporary operational environment. The research methodology section provides an overview to the material and case studies that following chapters will examine. First, it is important to identify the key research method and the primary research methodology of this thesis concentrates on qualitative research with an emphasis on content and discourse analysis. Qualitative research method is useful and an appropriate tool because most of this research focuses on comparing and examining different texts.

Under qualitative research methodology, case study method will provide an important tool to evaluate the evolution of Army doctrine since the publication of Kaldor's book (2012). The analysis will facilitate the tracing of key and instrumental changes from the pre-9/11 military concept such as Operations Other Than War (OOTW) to post Iraq and Afghanistan operations with the emerging doctrine of Strategic Landpower and the implantation of Army Doctrine 2015.

Case Studies Selection

This thesis will examine two different case studies to demonstrate the importance of understanding identity conflicts. The reason for choosing multiple case studies is that selecting only one case study might be insufficient and too narrowly drawn in understanding the larger context. This is very important when it comes to war and conflict. On other hand, too many case studies would simply be too burdensome as a research project of this nature. Thus, two case studies, drawn from different regions of the world, would be an appropriate choice for this thesis. Furthermore, each of the two case studies represents an important and relevant to the development of Army doctrine and how Army views identity conflicts, considering whether it is merely as an OOTW, an insurgency, or a broader and more serious character of war that should be given more thoughts and consideration in framing the current and perhaps future environment.

The first case study is the Bosnian conflict and the involvement from the United States military during Operation Joint Endeavor. Although the Bosnian conflict had started prior to the U.S. Army's direct engagement with the conflict, the purpose of this case study is not to go through each step of the conflict from the beginning to the end. Rather, the purpose of Bosnian case study illustrates how the U.S. Army had difficulty to operate under the existing framework, the 1993 version of FM 100-5, in an operational environment that it was not prepared for. Operation Joint Endeavor became an operation that lasted longer than most had initially expected. The Bosnian experience has provided a wealth of material and lessons learned for the U.S. Army in the development of FM 3-0 in 2001 (Kretchik 2011). Thus, it is a valuable for this thesis to evaluate this particular event.

The second case study is Operation Iraqi Freedom (OIF) from 2003 to 2008. Similar to the discussion in the previous case study, this thesis is not interested to go through every single event of the Second Iraq War, starting from the initial invasion in 2003, to the end. Rather, this thesis is interested in the tension and violence occurred amongst various ethnic groups. This is especially important between the Sunni and Shia during the peak of violence from 2005 to 2008 when countless innocent bystanders were killed. Furthermore, this case study also illustrates how the 2001 version of FM 3-0 was not capable of providing an adequate framework for the soldiers on the ground during this tumultuous period. This operational experience eventually led to the revision of FM 3-0, published in 2008.

Evaluation Criteria

The first criterion is the length of conflict, an aspect of "New Wars" theory. In each case study, one has to identify not only the historical linkages but also how these linkages have caused and triggered violence in places such as Bosnia and Iraq. In many instances, these historical linkages often are century-old and deep-rooted issues. In addition, it is important to look at the U.S. Army's length of participation in each operation to demonstrate the point that resolving an "identity conflict" requires the U.S. Army to conduct a longer and more sustained military operation. In this case, the standard is set at more than two years for this research study. It is a measurement created to prevent any misunderstanding between contingency operations and protracted military engagements.

The second criterion is to look at Army's operational experience. Individual experience on the ground, unit level AAR, and institutional level reflection are three categories to examine Army's operational experience. Furthermore, the U.S. Army's Combined Arms Center and Combat Studies Institute have conducted and maintained a collection of individual interviews, official studies, and unit AARs. In addition, news media outlets such as newspapers and television programs have also gathered a collection of materials that are useful for this research. Each interview, official publication or AAR provides an important perspective in understanding whether each level has experienced or witnessed "identity conflict" in each case study.

The third criterion is to examine Army's doctrinal development and change. More specifically, FM 100-5 (1993), FM 3-0 (2001), FM 3-0 (2008) are three critical documents in understanding how doctrinal change has evolved in the post-Cold War era. Furthermore, several unpublished drafts also provide important insights in doctrinal development and are instrumental in understanding whether Army has recognized "identity conflict" as a critical aspect of current environment. In all, these documents had served as the Army's keystone in explaining and determining how Army should operate.

Lastly, one has to examine the actual text of capstone doctrine, both the 2001 and 2008 versions of FM 3-0, to see whether these doctrines have recognized the identity conflict thesis. The key elements of the "New Wars" theory, provided in the literature review chapter, are the primary means to examine both the 2001 and 2008 version of FM 3-0. More specifically, Kaldor's three modes of warfare (2012), Münkler's state-disintegrating concept (2004), and Smith's "War Amongst the People" (2005) are three arguments that will examine whether Army's capstone doctrine has recognized the identity conflict thesis.

<u>Summary</u>

This chapter has identified qualitative research as the methodological process that this research project will use throughout this thesis to answer the primary and secondary research questions. In addition, Bosnia and Iraq are two case studies that will facilitate the discussion and the analysis of this research project. Furthermore, length of conflict, operational experience, doctrinal revision, and comparing the text of each published capstone doctrine with the "New Wars" theory are four evaluation criteria that will assess each case study to answer the primary question and secondary questions. This chapter has presented a methodological foundation for this research project, and the next section will begin to look at various empirical examples and start answering all the key questions for this thesis.

CHAPTER 4

ANALYSIS: BOSNIA AND THE 2001 FM 3-0

Introduction

The purpose of this chapter is to introduce the analysis of this thesis, beginning

with the U.S. Army's involvement in Bosnia to the publication of FM 3-0 in 2001. This

chapter begins with a short summary of U.S Army's involvement in the Bosnian conflict,

providing a short yet necessary context in framing the key discussion points later in this

chapter. Following the background section, this chapter examines the Bosnia conflict

through four evaluation criteria provided in the previous chapter. First, the length of

conflict will be discussed in both the local historical perspective and more importantly

the duration of American military involvement in the area. Secondly, operational

experience will largely be seen from individual experiences through interviews, unit level

AARs, and institutional level learning from sources such as official Army publications. It

is important to know whether the existing keystone manual at the time, the 1993 version

of FM 100-5, and this chapter traces the writing of new keystone manual from various

FM 100-5 revised drafts to the updated version of FM 3-0 in 2001. Lastly, it is important

to examine the final publication of FM 3-0 and to identify whether identity conflict has

become an important factor for the U.S. Army in its understanding of the contemporary

environment.

The Army's involvement in the Bosnia began with the signing of the Dayton

Peace Agreement in December 1995. As result of the peace agreement, the U.S. military

deployed its forces and began its peacekeeping operation in the northeast section of

Bosnia, covering places such as Tuzla, Brcko, Zupanja, and the infamous town place

Srebrenica. Operationally, the initial U.S. Army forces came from forces already stationed in Europe. Under the banner of Task Force Eagle, the First Armored Division, deployed with roughly about 11,000 personnel (Raugh 2010, 7). Task Force Eagle also included Russian, Turkish, and Norwegian units as well, making Task Force Eagle a multinational command. After the initial deployment of forces in December 1995, the U.S. Army chose to adopt a rotation method to continue its peacekeeping presence in Bosnia until 2004 when the United States officially declared end of mission. However, it is important to understand that the signing of the Dayton Accord and deployment of NATO forces did not necessarily mean the end of hostility. In short, some observed that "the struggle just took on a different form with the entry of NATO . . . warring factions were all naturally disposed to test the resolve of IFOR and its successor" (Baumann, Gawrych, and Kretchik 2004, 124). Serbians, Bosnian Muslims, and Croatians were all vying to gain an advantage during the peacekeeping operation. This type of complex scenario presented a challenge for the U.S. Army to confront how it should operate in an uncertain world.

Length of Conflict

The U.S. Army's involvement in Bosnia official began in 1995 and ended in 2004. However, the actual conflict in Bosnia, in its most recent episode, started in 1992 when Slovenia, Croatia, and Bosnia broke away from the Socialist Federal Republic of Yugoslavia. Robert Kaplan's book, *Balkan Ghosts: A Journal Through History*, provides a historical analysis of this region and its contemporary issues, detailing a synopsis of the Balkan conflict and tracing how religious and ethnic tensions have played an important factor in this part of the world (1993). The operational environment on the ground has clearly illustrated the prolonged nature of the conflict in Bosnia. It fits well with one of

Münkler's (2004) key characteristics of the "New Wars" theory

Operationally, the length of conflict also plays a factor for the U.S. Army as well.

It presents itself as another challenge to the existing structure that was struggling to come

with the term that this type of operation is going last longer than expected, a point that

directly supports Münkler's analysis on the duration of conflict. For example, Anthony

Cucolo, an infantry battalion commander during Operation Joint Endeavor in 1996 and

most recently served as the Commandant of U.S. Army War College, told a journalist

that "Peacekeeping is a very undefined mission. There's no terrain that has to be taken,

no object to be seized. Right now I'm feeling that I'm leaving here with the mission only

half-completed" (Hundley 1996). The notion that one deployment is sufficient to

complete the mission was simply not possible in the new environment and this statement

serves as an example that many Army officers had problem coping with multiple

deployments to the same area working on the same problem. In short, the length of

conflict in Bosnia, from the perspective of the U.S. Army's involvement, was longer than

other types of military operation, comparing it with operation in Grenada, Panama, and

Operation Desert Shield/Storm.

<u>Operational Experiences</u>

Operational experience in Bosnia can be described by looking at three different

levels. Each level offers a different viewpoint in answering the primary and secondary

research questions. The first perspective looks at different individual reflection on the

events occurred during this period. These individual reflections can range from foot

soldiers on the ground to the command general responsible for the entire area of operation. The second perspective looks at unit level reflection by examining the AAR. The purpose is to examine a collective group's experience in Bosnia at the tactical level. Lastly, the third perspective looks at the institutional level reflection. More specifically, this thesis is interested in how the U.S. Army examined its own actions in Bosnia.

Individual experiences

Individual experiences in Bosnia account for an important and valuable aspect of many lessons learned in the overall all operational experience in dealing with conflict after the end of the Cold War. Although the U.S. military had engaged in this type of operations in Somalia and Haiti, Bosnia was the first sustained military operation in support of OOTW. These individual experiences will clearly illustrate the frustration with the existing doctrine and way to approach military operation in a new era.

At the individual level, many participants have identified some characteristics of the "New Wars" theory in Bosnia. For example, one interview indicates, "[in Bosnia] money was a driver more than any ideology . . . it was more about who had the money, who had the control, who was in power to make the decision" (Belcher 2012). This particular experience from an Army officer served in Bosnia illustrates the influence of both the role of non-state actors and war financing mechanism in Bosnia. This also supports Kaldor's analysis on the Bosnia conflict and her "New Wars" theory (2012). The role of non-state actors is a key divergent point between Kaldor (2012) and the U.S. Army (1993) in how each understands and interprets the contemporary operational environment.

Some of these operational experiences also express the perspective that the 1993 version of FM 100-5 and the overall military thinking and doctrines were not sufficient in dealing with situation in places like Bosnia. Some officers expressed the frustration that

"the idea that proficiency in battle drills will automatically equate to proficiency in nation

building, negotiation and dealing with things less than full combat is just flat wrong"

(Dempsey 2007). To focus more exclusively within the realm of doctrine, this type of

sentiment amongst junior officers demonstrates as a frustration that the existing doctrine

could not provide a satisfactory guide for these officers to operation in Bosnia.

In short, individual operational experiences in Bosnia clearly demonstrate that a

different kind of war and conflict does exist. Traditional military power and thinking

could not adequately confront many of these new challenges. In addition, some of the

participants clearly expressed their views that the U.S. Army did not have an adequate

doctrinal base to provide a useful framework for its forces to deal with a kind of war.

Unit AARs

Unit level AARs are focusing both at the tactical and operational levels. Although

many of these AARs focused on internal operational procedures and ways to improve for

future operations, there are key lessons learned that valuable to understand how the post-

Cold War environment presented these units with different challenges. In this section, 1st

Battalion, 41st Infantry's (1-41 IN 1997) AAR from its deployment in support of

Operation Joint Endeavor in 1997 is an example that illustrates how the U.S. Army, at the

unit level, had to adapt to the environment on the ground. Furthermore, this section also

demonstrates that tactical units had confronted the issue of identity conflict, particularly

in separating different ethnic groups during the peacekeeping phase. Lastly, this section

looks at the V Corps' AAR, from an operational perspective, in 1996 as a way to examine

whether a higher-level command shared a similar view as its subordinate units.

At the tactical level, one of the first lessons learned is a lack of clarity in understanding the mission in Bosnia. From 1-41 IN's experience, a lack of clarity and understanding in the overall mission resulted "no indication of impending Peace Enforcement Operations and the mission was not contained in its Mission Essential Task List" (1-41 IN 1997: II-1). This confusion translated to a lack of clarity during 1-41 IN's preparation phase while training at its home-station. For example, 1-41 IN had to adopt three new and revised METL based on its mission: "Enforce the General Framework Agreement for Peace, Deter Hostilities, and Promote Stability" (1-41 IN 1997, II-3). From these tasks, 1-41 IN conducted missions such as assisting arms reductions, checkpoint operations, and promoting economic growth through the assistance of International and Non-Governmental Organizations (1-41 IN 1997, II-5). While some of these METLs might seem obvious today because of U.S. Army's experience in Iraq and Afghanistan, 1-41 IN, with little training and experience in stability operations, adapted to the situation on the ground and formulated a coherent mission statement that was suitable in dealing with a complex and post-conflict environment.

In addition, 1-41 IN had a good demographic awareness that translated to its thoughtful operational approach throughout its deployment. For example, 1-41 IN clearly understood that its Area of Operation consists of "evenly divided between Bosniaks and Serbs, with a small population of Croats concentrated near the town of Vares" (1-41 IN 1997, II-2). Although this appears as merely basic background information on the breakdown of different ethnic groups in the region, this information was highly important to 1-41 IN and its leadership because the deep historical issues and troubled past that resulted in a modern conflict among various ethnic groups. 1-41 IN accurately captured

41

the diversity of its area in its analysis and utilized this information to implement positive

changes. For example, 1-41 IN and its leadership understood the level of unemployment

in the region as a "cause for concern" in maintaining peace amongst various ethnic

groups (1-41 IN 1997, II-2). Demonstrating an ability to look beyond the conventional

model, 1-41 IN and its leadership clearly understood some of the underlying causes of

violence in the region. Furthermore, units like 1-41 IN also knew how these causes could

worsen the ethnic tension in a fragile, post-conflict environment. In all, 1-41 IN's

experience in Bosnia demonstrates that tactical level units were dealing with situations

that required creative and critical thinking. 1-41 IN confronted and witnessed many of the

characteristics of "New Wars" theory firsthand while trying to enforce a mandate to

maintain peace in a post-conflict, violence-ridden country.

At the operational level, the V Corps AAR, conducted in 1996, offers very little

discussion on V Corp's operational lessons in Bosnia (Raugh 2010, 277-286). Rather this

AAR focused on logistical support, deployment capability, morale consideration, and

other elements that had little to do with conducting a peacekeeping mission (Raugh 2010,

277-286). The V Corps AAR concentrated on the organizational level issues because V

Corps, as an operational headquarter, provided an administrative function to operational

units in Bosnia. As a reflection, V Corps' AAR is a vivid illustration of a persisted failure

within the U.S. Army in understanding the evolving nature of a changing environment

since the end of Cold War.

The two examples offer a contrasting view and perhaps disconnect between the

tactical level observation and operational level in understanding the operational

environment in Bosnia. On the one hand, tactical units, like 1-41 IN, had identified issues on the ground that required a different kind of thinking and solution. On the other hand, operational command, like V Corps, had a difficult time in understanding the operational environment in Bosnia because it only focused on the administrative side.

Institutional Reflection

As an institution, the U.S. Army recorded and documented many lessons learned from its operation in Bosnia. The U.S. Army's Combat Studies Institute (CSI) conducted several studies into Army's experience in Bosnia. There are many key themes coming out of these studies. However, CSI did not complete many of these studies until the Bosnian mission had ended. Nonetheless, these official studies still offer a valuable glimpse into the overall organizational experience during this period. Moreover, many of the findings from these studies echo many characteristics of the "New Wars" theory and validate the identity conflict thesis. Yet, the majority of the lessons learned focuses heavily on Army's ability to conduct rapid deployment with a sustainable force on the ground.

First, the analysis focuses on the chaotic nature in the pre-operational planning within the military organization and staff prior to the execution of Operation Joint Endeavor (Baumann, Gawrych, and Kretchik 2004, chapter 3). Amid this chaos, the analysis captures the confusion amongst UN, NATO, and U.S. military planners to properly plan and implement the actual execution of the Dayton Peace Accord through deployment of military forces to Bosnia. The CSI study argues that, "in truth, no plan could match Bosnian realities precisely, for political and military conditions changed continually" (Baumann, Gawrych, and Kretchik 2004, 71). This reflection is a good examination of the complex situation on the ground. Despite a signed peace accord amongst all belligerents, the operational environment remained very fluid. Yet, the Army was not able to act decisively in the initial stage of the operation.

In addition to some of the shortcomings during the initial stage, the CSI studies also captures the difficulty in resolving the existing conflict under a tenuous framework provided for NATO forces to operate in Bosnia. In short, the CSI argues that "the war failed to end the ethnic conflict; the struggle just took on a different form with the entry of NATO" (Baumann, Gawrych, and Kretchik 2004, 124). This assessment offers a perspective into the challenges on the ground that U.S. forces had to deal with in order to maintain peace in a complex operational environment. The analysis also points out that soldiers on the ground became well versed in diffusion the tension "by judiciously balancing negotiation with intimidation, depending on circumstances" (Baumann, Gawrych, Kretchik 2004, 126). In short, the Army fully understood that it has the advantage of military hardware and technology as its advantage in dealing with the ethnic tension on the ground. For example, the commander of Task Force Eagle would use satellite imagery to show local militia commanders how they directly violated the peace accord and forced them to withdraw (Baumann, Gawrych, and Kretchik 2004, 125). In addition, there are many examples recounting various checkpoint operations and their difficult in separating various ethnic factions. In all, the CSI studies accurately picks up the ethnic tension on the ground and how the U.S. military was able to deal with this tenuous peace through leveraging its strength and creative thinking.

Through individual, unit, institutional reflects, there are many examples that clearly illustrated the existing FM 100-5 was not capable of coping with the operational environment in places such as Bosnia. As a result, the Army had to re-evaluate its capstone manual and begin drafting a new version.

Doctrinal Evolution: Creation of FM 3-0

As an update to Army's initial post-Cold War capstone manual, FM 3-0 was designed to be a "transitional doctrine" (Kretchik 2011, 248). Walter Kretchik's *U.S. Army Doctrine: From the American Revolution to the War on Terror* discusses the ideological struggle within the U.S. Army from the 1993 version of FM 100-5 to the 2001 version of FM 3-0, focusing on multiple attempts to revise the manual under several different leaders (2011, 221-262). Within this doctrinal development process, this research project focuses on the part of capstone manual that discusses the contemporary operational environment.

Initial Attempts in 1997 and 1998

Prior to the publication of FM 3-0 in 2001, two earlier drafts were circulated within the U.S. Army in 1997 and 1998. Each draft contains a different philosophical idea. Walter Kretchik's book offers a thorough discussion on the background of each draft and the personality conflict occurred during the drafting process (2011). Both proposed revision have contained a more advanced and mature thinking about the post-Cold War environment than the existing capstone doctrine, the 1993 version of FM 100-5.

In the 1997 draft version of FM 100-5, a clear positioned was established to paint a picture about "the nature of modern conflict" (US Army 1997: I-2-1). In this draft version of Army capstone manual, there seems to be a nuance understanding about the complexity of the post-Cold War environment. First, this draft spells out that "the objective in committing military force is often resolution of a conflict . . . at the strategic level, ending a particular conflict does not end all conflict" (US Army 1997: I-2-2). This expresses one of the key points by Münkler in the "New Wars" theory about the length of conflict in the contemporary world. It is quite clear that the writers of this draft had a good grasp of the characteristics of the contemporary environment and thoughtfully inserted the section about the duration and the length of conflict. At the same time, the 1997 draft version also many of the key Clausewitz ideas such as friction, change and uncertainty. In the same section that describes the nature of modern conflict, the 1997 draft version of FM 100-5 specifically mentions that "friction plaques every effort to resolve conflict" (US Army 1997: I-2-4). It seems that there was an attempt to account and address for the changing environment. Yet, the 1997 draft was discarded due to leadership changes and philosophical differences at the highest level (Kretchik 2011, 244-5).

The 1998 draft version of FM 100-5, a different approach from the 1997 draft, still contains many of the existence thinking and ideas about the post-Cold War environment. Furthermore, this draft did not address the issue of identity conflict even though the U.S. Army had already operated in Bosnia for almost three years at this point. Rather the 1998 draft created the term "AirLand Dominance" as a new approach to address the strategic environment (US Army 1998). AirLand Dominance is defined as "Army forces achieve and sustain AirLand Dominance over forces, terrain, populations, and production capabilities by seizing, maintaining, and exploiting the initiative . . . characterized by simultaneous operations executed by aggressive, disciplined, and versatile forces employing superior military means" (US Army 1998, 21). Within this draft version, Army tried to capture the essence of the current land forces debate and address full range of Army action while retaining warfighting as its principle focus (US Army 1998, 22). It is rather clear that this particular version of the draft puts an emphasis on the traditional way of warfare in which military is a primary means to conduct state on state type of conflict.

As a departure from the previous FM 100-5, the 1998 draft initiated the usage of Offensive, Defensive, Stability and Support as four types of military operation. This is a step away from the previous concept of thinking military operations in terms of war or OOTW. By using these newly created categories, one can combine all four types of operation in a single military operation. Thus, it is an important recognition that a major combat operation can also contain elements of stability and support operations as well. The acknowledgement that a major combat operation can contain different elements demonstrates a more insightful draft that tries to understand the contemporary operational environment.

The Final Version

The FM 3-0 in 2001 represents a significant shift from the 1993 version of FM 100-5, not only in its new numerical title but also in its updated content and thinking behind how to best understand and deal with the world that has evolved from the Cold War era and slowly morphed into a new and different environment. There are several important changes in the 2001 FM 3-0. First, the concept of "Full Spectrum Operations," covering offense, defense, stability, and support operations, marks as a distinct and noticeable departure from the 1993 FM 100-5 on dealing with the contemporary global environment (US Army 2001). The previous section mentions that the 1998 draft of FM 100-5 had already incorporated stability and support as two additional military operations that the Army has to consider in its thinking. The publication of FM 3-0 finalized and solidified the inclusion of stability and support as part of the Full Spectrum concept. Under the "Full Spectrum" concept, the Army is ready to conduct operations across the wide spectrum ranging from major theater war to peacetime military engagement (see figure 2). By combining offense, defense, stability, and support operations in a joint, multinational, and interagency environment, the U.S Army believes it is the formula for mission accomplishment (US Army 2001, 1-16). In short, full spectrum operation is the Army's answer to confront the contemporary operational environment.

Despite the creation of full spectrum concept, there is still a separation between war and MOOTW, OOTW's latest revision. After all, war represents, according to Army's own definition, major theater war and MOOTW is defined operations deterring war, resolving conflict, and promoting peace (US Army 2001, 1-15). Army's focus remains on an offensive mindset as defined by General Eric Shinseki's emphasis that "first we win on the offense; we must be able to defend well, but you win on the offense" (US Army 2001, Foreword). The emphasis on offensive operations clearly suggests that fighting a major theater war as more important than MOOTW or operation that does not involve a conventional war between regular militaries.

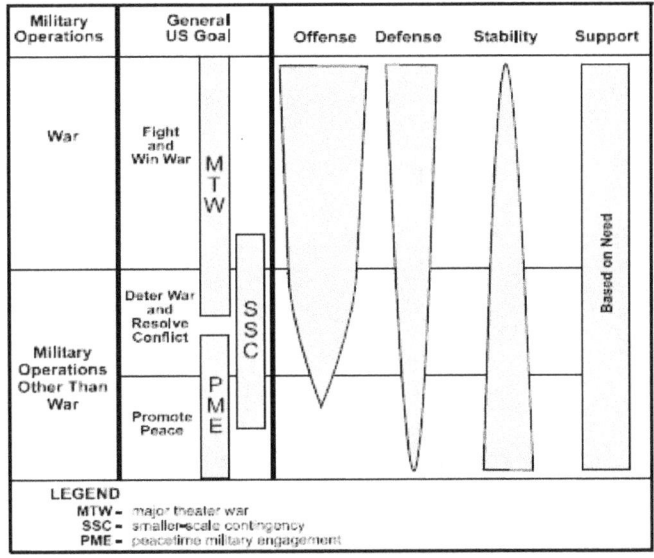

Figure 2.   FM 3-0 Range of Military Operations

Source: Department of the Army, Field Manual (FM) 3-0, *Operations* (Washington, DC: Government Printing Office, 2001), 1-15.

In addition to the Full Spectrum concept, another important aspect is the

discussion on strategic responsiveness in chapter three. The whole idea centers on "Army

forces trained, organized, and equipped for global operations . . . proficient at force

projection" (US Army 2001, 3-0). This is an important lesson learned coming from the

Balkan experience. As previously discussed in the operational experience section, the

inability to quickly deploy forces to Bosnia was one of key lesson learned and the newly

developed capstone manual tries to maintain the focus by highlighting this issue.

Furthermore, this chapter also coincided with the development of interim force, a lighter

and more agile unit that could be deployed more rapidly. Listing various attributes of a

strategically responsive force, the manual identifies key areas such as responsive,

deployable, agile, versatile, lethal, survivable, and sustainable (US Army 2001, 3-1). In short, this is an effort to energize the organizational effort to ensure the Army remains as a relevant military force.

Another key point to emphasize is the revision to the mission variables from METT-T (Mission, Enemy, Terrain, Troops, and Time) to METT-TC (Civil Consideration) (US Army 2001, 5-3). The inclusion of civil consideration marks as an important step in the institutional understanding of the contemporary environment. It sends an important signal that military has to evaluate its operation with civilian as a criteria in its calculus. Although this is not the same as "War Amongst the People" (Smith 2005), adding civil consideration as a part of Army's mission variable demonstrates an attempt to capture the lessons in Bosnia and offers a way to include this variable as a comprehensive approach in addressing military operation. Yet, this revision did not go beyond the mission variable. For example, the manual lists threat, political, unified action, land combat operations, information, and technology as dimensions of an operational environment (US Army 2001, 1-8). There is no mention of human factor as a possible dimension. Thus, the incorporation of civil consideration in the mission variable is not an insignificant step and it does provide a useful framework for the forces to understand and consider the human factor, at least at the tactical level operations.

Does FM 3-0 recognize identity conflict as a feature of war?

The 2001 FM 3-0, while it maintains mostly Clausewitzian ideas, has also contained some of the core principles of the "New Wars" theory. Overall, it still sides, overwhelmingly, with the traditional concept of warfare. In addition, the 2001 FM 3-0 did not adequately address many of the key issues in the Bosnia experience, neglecting some of the important lessons learned and continuing the path of focusing on the next evolution of the doctrinal change rather a complete revolution. In the end, the 2001 version of FM 3-0 represents an attempt to consider the identity conflict argument, through Army's experience in the Balkans, but the this capstone doctrine still lacks many of the important features that are critical in understanding this dynamic and ever-changing environment.

One of the key elements, in recognizing identity conflict as a feature war and violence, is to see whether the doctrine has incorporated any of the "New Wars" theory in its context. Kaldor's argument (2012), largely based on her analysis of the Bosnian conflict, has reflected very little in the 2001 version of FM 3-0 except in one section that describes the threat dimension. This section mentions that "extremism, ethnic disputes, religious rivalries, and human disasters contribute to huge refugee migrations . . . threat to the environment and a region's stability . . . may adversely affect US interest" (US Army 2001, 1-8). There is a minimal recognition of ethnic and religious strife could potential destabilize a region and US interest. There is very little discussion on the complexity of these types of conflict, primarily originated from identity difference among different groups with long historical past.

Furthermore, the manual focuses too exclusively on adversary's action against the American military without giving a more thoughtful consideration about the overall operational environment in its entirety. For example, the manual mentions that "adversaries will also seek to shape conditions to their advantage . . . use capabilities that they believe difficult for US forces to counter . . . to offset US advantages" (US Army 2001, 1-9). The manual's emphasis on countering enemy actions is not unimportant, but the discussion on the larger operational environment should be more thorough in its thinking and analysis. Kaldor's "New Wars" theory describes three relevant characteristics of the contemporary warfare and conflict based on a study of recent conflicts (2012). However, FM 3-0 seems to extract different sets of lessons learned and the two have very little in common. Thus, one cannot say that there is any coherent agreement or similarity between the two writings.

As far as understanding the protracted nature and state-disintegrating features, the 2001 FM 3-0 offers only a very limited perspective in its explanation. Rather, the manual focuses on the quick mobilization, forcible entry, dominate land operations, and support civil authority during the transition (US Army 2001, 1-4). There seems to be a concentration on the ability to quickly deploy, complete the mission, and get out as soon as possible. Thus, it is important to plan in a scenario where Army can get in and get out rapidly without considering and factoring the nature of conflict on the ground. The only portion of the manual that talks about the protracted nature of conflict is in the discussion on principles of war in which the manual mentions that "offensive and defensive operations may swiftly create the conditions for short-term success, but protracted stability operations or support operation may be needed to cement lasting strategic objectives" (US Army 2001, 4-12). This is a good description in the utility of stability operation to shape the outcome of a conflict. Yet, this is not an important aspect of the 2001 FM 3-0. The doctrine primarily focuses on the speediness of deployment, win and redeployment. Thus, there is very little agreement between the doctrine and Münkler's argument. Therefore, one cannot say that the doctrine recognizes this aspect of the "New Wars" theory and the associated identity conflict thesis.

Lastly, the FM 3-0 does not address the issue of "war amongst the people" as a feature in contemporary warfare and conflict. There is nothing in the manual that discusses the operational environment where people should be considered as a factor. In describing the operational environment, threat, political, unified action, land combat operations, information, and technology are the components (US Army 2001, 1-8). There is no mention about the human domain. Essentially, this is an enemy-centric focus manual in its analysis about the operational environment with very limited discussion how human factor can play an integral role. This is a clear gap in linking the actual experience on the ground in places like Bosnia with how the Army thinks the key components of operational environment should be. In short, Smith's thesis is partially derived from Bosnia and it is interesting to see that there is a clear different in how the Army has failed to capture this key point.

In all, the 2001 FM 3-0 tries to conceptualize the post-Cold War environment through an updated explanation. Yet, the experience in Bosnia has clearly shown that identity conflict has become an important feature of the contemporary warfare and conflict. However, the manual fails to address this aspect and continues to focus on the conventional warfare as if the only purpose of Army is to fight another world war with a near peer competitive. The desire to resolve issue in this complex environment turned into a laser light focus to deploy faster and quicker. This kind of thinking can be represented in some of the military literatures in which the focus has been placed on power projection capability (see Wass de Czege and Echevarria, 2000). Rather than understand the complexity of the operational environment, this focus did lead to the creation of interim force and Stryker vehicle as a solution, but equipment and organizational changes cannot replace a faulty doctrinal thinking in its understanding about the world. In short, the 2001 FM 3-0 does contain many thoughtful changes, but this manual does not recognize the identity conflict as an important character to contemporary warfare and conflict.

Summary

The Bosnia case study shows that the U.S. Army had discovered the 1993 FM 100-5's limitation. Although the manual, published at the end of the Cold War, had attempted to provide a framework for the Army to operation in a changing operational environment, the doctrine was not sufficient to meet the actual challenge on the ground in places such as Bosnia. The conflict in Bosnia has an ancient root and it was worsen with the breakup of Yugoslavia. The dynamic amongst the Bosnian Muslim, Croatians, and Serbians was tenuous at best during the Cold War. This tension was shattered first by the breakup of Slovenia and Croatia and the subsequent breakup of Bosnia further triggered a wave of violence that included the genocide committed in the town of Srebrenica by Serbian militia targeting unarmed Bosnia Muslim women and children. Responding to an international outcry, the world community finally responded with force, which ended with the signing of Dayton Peace Accord and deployment of peacekeeping forces to Bosnia. The U.S. Army began its involvement in late 1995 and finally ended its mission in 2004. Through this extended military operation, it has shown that an identity conflict, such as in Bosnia, has not only a prolonged history but requires a long commitment, on all fronts, in order to maintain the peace.

The operational experience in Bosnia has demonstrated that the Army encountered a different type of operation and some of the units were not prepared at first to operate in the new environment. Although many of the feedbacks, from individual to institutional reflection, have clearly illustrated that identity conflict as an important feature, much of discussions have centered on Army's ability rapidly deploys to a region and the ability to sustain that operation. Although some of reflections and lessons learned led to the creation of an interim force, with Stryker vehicles as the centerpiece, in order to deploy a mobile force quicker to a region, the actual lesson on the messiness of a complex environment was missed when the focus surrounded the development of this interim force as a solution to all problems. It is unfortunate that the evidences are there to show that identity conflict should be considered as a cause for this violence, but this is not captured as a main lesson within the institution.

As early as 1995, the Army recognized that the existing capstone doctrine, FM 100-5, needed another revision. With actual operational experience and lesson learned from Bosnia and other places, there were multiple attempts to revise the doctrine. The attempts in 1997 and 1998 reflected an inconsistent effort to create a coherent argument that is acceptable at all levels. Yet, there are many valuable concepts in these earlier drafts that accurately reflect the complexity of the post-Cold War operational environment. The eventual publication of the FM 3-0 in 2001 represents years of effort to create a coherent argument and guide the Army forces in a dynamic world. From the full spectrum concept to

Comparing the published FM 3-0 with the "New Wars" theory, one can see that the doctrine has recognized very limited aspects of identity conflict as a feature in contemporary warfare and conflict. However, the overwhelming portion of the doctrine continues to emphasize the tradition concept of warfare as reflected by its concentration on Clausewitz ideas and thinking. Furthermore, there seems to be a gap between the actual lessons learned on the ground in Bosnia and the published doctrine. This shortfall will become problematic in the next chapter of this study. Some Army leaders have declared this doctrine as "not Cold War doctrine . . . not even post-Cold War doctrine. It looks forward" (Steele 2001). This is a problematic statement with many flaws because the fact that this updated version did not accurately capture the operational environment and offer a viable framework for soldiers on the ground to resolve a complex problem. In short, this doctrine does not fully concur with the "New Wars" theory argument and its associated identity conflict thesis as a feature in the contemporary warfare and conflict.

In all, the Bosnia experience illustrates Army's attempt to confront an international crisis, with an identity conflict as its origin. The U.S. Army failed to adequately capture and incorporate many of lessons learned into its updated capstone doctrine. The notion that Bosnia was merely a peacekeeping operation with little relevance to the conventional warfare led to a missed opportunity for the U.S. Army to fully comprehend the dynamic situation on the ground. Furthermore, the failure to see how an ethnic divide, triggering a deep-rooted hatred and chaotic environment, can exacerbate the existing order and fragile stability, which could lead to an application of additional military operations in a more aggressive manner at the cost of creating a post-conflict order. The 2001 version of FM 3-0 represents both as a missed opportunity for the entire Army and an inaccurate understanding in the complexity and disorderliness of the operational environment. This deficiency has its consequence and the next chapter will look at Army's struggle in Iraq to confront a complex environment with an inadequate doctrine on hand.

CHAPTER 5

ANALYSIS: IRAQ AND THE 2008 FM 3-0

Introduction

This chapter examines how the Iraq experience has influenced the 2008 version of FM 3-0. The flow of this chapter follows the basic structure as the previous chapter. However, it is important to recognize that there are some key differences between Bosnia and Iraq. Firstly, OIF was an operation designed to remove Saddam Hussein from power through conducting an offensive operation. As a result, the intensity of combat was much higher in Iraq than in Bosnia, which was a relatively non-violent operation. The intensity of violence marks as the most significant contrast between the two operations. Secondly, there was a higher level of national attention and awareness on the events in Iraq. To this day, OIF remains as a divisive issue in America. Despite its unique status, one can still examine whether the Army has properly adapted to a complex operational environment and recognized that identity conflict as a cause that led to sectarian unrest and instability throughout the country.

This section is not going to dwell and reinvestigate all the specific events in OIF. There is a plethora of materials that cover many different angles and perspectives (Rick 2006, 2009; Filkins 2009; Packer 2006; Gordon and Trainor 2006, 2012; Chandrasekaran 2006; West 2008). In addition, the U.S. Army's official publications such as *On Point I* (Fontenot et al. 2004) and *On Point II* (Wright et al. 2008) have also examined many critical events in Iraq and some of the important lessons learned. Rather than repeating the same historical chronology, this section chooses to review only key events that led to the upsurge of sectarian violence and key turning points that would enable the discussion on the inadequacy of 2001 version of FM 3-0 and the revision of 2008 version of FM 3-0.

Immediately after the fall of Baghdad, the U.S. military suffered a series of setbacks, which resulted in instability in many key areas and a public consensus that questioned America's ability to handle a growing insurgency. Under this context, groups such as Abu Musab al-Zarqawi's Al Qaeda in Iraq (AQIZ) and Muqtada al-Sadr's Mahdi Army (JAM) exploited the existing ethnic and sectarian tensions amongst different groups. The sectarian attacks kept rising to the point that some experts have called it "the war after the war" (Cordesman 2006, 7). Finally, the bombing of Al-Askari Mosque, the third holiest Shia shrine, in February 2006 became the boiling point that triggered an unstoppable wave of violence across the country (BBC 2006). This wave of violence was so destructive that it eventually caused the Bush Administration to change its strategy in Iraq and select General David Petraeus as the new commander to confront this urgent situation (Woodward 2006; Woodward 2008). It is under this context that this research examines whether identity conflict in Iraq has influenced the revision of the U.S. Army capstone doctrine, FM 3-0, published in 2008.

<u>Length of Conflict</u>

Like Bosnia, Iraq, too, has a long history filled with tension and violence amongst the Sunni, Shia, and Kurds lasted far longer than the formation of modern state. Some of scholarship that is more recent tries to analyze the effect of the post-Saddam Iraq has on the dynamic between the Sunni and Shia with an emphasis that the conflict between these two groups will shape the formation of Middle East (Nasr 2006). There are plenty of literatures that examine the long struggle between these two groups (see Lewis 1997;

Mansfield 1991). Furthermore, the purpose of this section is not to retrace the origins of schism, but to simply recognize the profound history behind it. In short, the dynamic in Iraq, or more specifically the Mesopotamia region, fits the definition of the "New Wars" theory very well as far as its protracted struggle amongst different groups. In modern time, the U.S. Army has also a long involvement in Iraq and its ethnic struggle, dating back to the initial aftermath of the Operation Desert Storm when the U.S. had to send military forces to Northern Iraq and provide a safe haven for the Kurdish people against Saddam Hussein's retribution. Operation Provide Comfort and later became Operation Northern Watch were military operations designed to safeguard the Kurdish population in northern Iraq against Saddam Hussein's regime by establishing a no-fly zone. A similar no-fly zone was established in the southern portion as well as result of Saddam's retribution toward to the Shia population. These operations finally ended in 2003 when OIF began.

Following the initial stages in OIF, the U.S. thought it could pull out rather quickly after the fall of Baghdad, but the failure in some of the initial reconstruction efforts forced the U.S. to reconsider its position and began a long and protracted involvement to stabilize a fragile state. From the often-criticized "Mission Accomplished" sign displaying over the deck of USS Abraham Lincoln, the U.S. could not fully grasp the complexity in Iraq and this folly continued to plaque the overall effort to stabilize a country that was slowly getting out of control under a rising Sunni insurgency. In the end, OIF transitioned to Operation New Dawn in 2010 and all American forces withdraw from Iraq on December, 2011. The pullout from Iraq was not permanent because the Obama administration, as result of rising Sunni insurgency operating under the banner of Islamic State, has recommitted military forces to fight against an old nemesis.

The history has shown that the conflict in Iraq, whether it is the internal sectarian struggle amongst different ethnic groups lasting over hundreds of years or a more simplistic view of West versus Islam, will continue for the near future because many of the fundamental issues have not been resolved. Looking from the perspective of the "New Wars" theory, the struggle in Iraq represents a "state-disintegrating" conflict with the Sunni and Kurds wanting to separate from the Shia led government. Sectarian identity becomes a key issue in causing each group to commit violence against others. This long and enduring conflict would likely to continue if there is no active attempt to resolve some of the fundamental difference amongst different groups through a coherent political process.

Operational Experiences in Iraq

The collective operational experience in Iraq constitutes as a critical and insightful perspective in understanding the contemporary environment. Furthermore, these experiences also offer a firsthand account on how identity conflict has permeated throughout Iraq. In discussing this section, one has to be cognizant about equating the Bosnia or Kosovo operations with Iraq because there are many differences. Moreover, the Army had committed a much larger portion of its forces, along with the U.S. Marine Corps, to OIF with forces engaged in high intensity combat operations in places such as Ramadi, Fallujah, Samarra, Tel Afar, Sadr City, and Baqubah. Through these firsthand accounts in Iraq, it is quite clear that, after the initial invasion and the failure to achieve stability, Iraq disintegrated into a seemingly unstoppable sectarian violence primarily between the Sunni and Shia. This section looks at both individual interviews and institutional reflections to gauge whether these sources have clearly demonstrated whether identity conflict was present in Iraq.

Individual experiences

As part of gathering institutional knowledge, there is ample and abundant of information available from this period. The Combined Arms Center at Fort Leavenworth, Kansas has created an archive full of interviews with operational experiences in Iraq. In addition, a multitude of interviews conducted through various news media also add to the collection of individual experiences in Iraq. From all these sources, one can pull important interviews to illustrate some of the important lessons learned and shortcomings during the earlier portion of the OIF. Interviews from the military practitioners will demonstrate some of major challenges in Iraq and the existing thinking about how to deal with insurgency was incapable of confronting a dynamic environment.

Recognizing that Iraq as a different environment from previous operations is an important first step, many of the personal experiences in Iraq reflected a challenging operational environment on the ground. From some, the environment is defined as "a hybrid enemy . . . combination of former regime people who benefitted from Saddam, and also Islamic extremist . . . over time, this decentralized hybrid insurgency has sort of [evolved], and there have been alliances of convenience" (McMaster 2005). In addition to a hybrid Sunni insurgency in northern Iraq, another perspective also shows the complexity of multiple insurgent activities throughout the country in 2004 "when violence broke out all over the country, incited by Moqtada al-Sadr's military . . . also by Sunni-Arab insurgents, whose actions included the hanging of contractors in the city of

Fallujah" (Petraeus 2006, 3). From Petraeus' perspective, one can clearly see the dynamic of multiple insurgencies creating chaos throughout the country where there was very little stability and lack of governance to properly address this issue. Lastly, operating in an urbanized slum such as Sadr City, a Shia dominated town where there was little basic services and a large population with high unemployment, exposes the difficulty to apply conventional military means to address an unconventional problem (Chiarelli and Michaelis 2005). These personal reflections illustrate the intricacy and multidimensional aspect of a post-conflict environment. Within this operational environment, other reflections will recall the identity conflict occurred amongst different groups, all fighting for its share and stake in a post Saddam Iraq.

Across many different practitioners, all were aware of tension between the Sunni and the Shia. Not long after the fall of Baghdad and capture of Saddam Hussein, insurgent activities became prevalent throughout the country and some elements began exploiting the tension amongst different ethnic and sectarian groups. Some have understood this tension quite well in knowing "the most extreme Al Qaeda true believers viewed Shia as apostates . . . they were happy to participate in what they saw as revenge attacks against the Shia whom they saw as their enemies" (Yingling 2006, 14). This kind of observation is not isolated because there are others also observed this kind of violence amongst various groups. For example, some military commanders commenting on the attack of Al-Askari Mosque in 2006 by the predominant Sunni group AQIZ as "threw gas on an already existing fire" (MacFarland 2008, 15). In short, these observations illustrate that the tension amongst different groups was worsen after the fall of Saddam and this increase of violence ultimately led to a sectarian conflict, primarily between the Sunni and Shia, growing out of control.

Another key point from these interviews is the necessity to use "informal practice" as a way to confront the complex environment on the ground. There are many examples to illustration this point. The first example is the First Calvary Division's attempt to operate successfully with Sadr City in 2004 through a mixture of restoring essential services while conducting military operations to defeat Shia insurgency, primarily sponsored by the Mahdi Army (Chiarelli and Michaelis 2005). In this particular example, the First Calvary Division adopted framework focusing on areas such as sewer, water, electricity, employment, trash, and governance as a means to gain the support from the populace and deny insurgent influence (Chiarelli and Michaelis 2005, 10). This is a highly successful concept and the model has been transitioned into an acronym SWEAT-MS (Sewage, Water, Electricity, Academics, Trash, Medical, and Safety) as an assessment tool to better understand the operational environment at the tactical level. Yet, this represents the needs for commanders and soldiers to develop a non-standard type solution in a complex environment.

Another example is the case of Third Armored Calvary Regiment's (3rd ACR) deployment in 2005 under the leadership of its commander, H.R. McMaster. 3rd ACR is a good example to show a tactical unit's effort to deal with a complex through ingenuity. Also, this is an example that demonstrates the failure of existing doctrine to satisfactorily answer to needs of the soldiers on the ground. In preparing for its soldier for the deployment, the unit had to "learn . . . from the experience in Iraq between 2003 and 2004 and then apply those lessons" (McMaster 2007). From this careful study of previous experience, the plan of "clear, hold, and build" was created as a framework to deal with insurgency in the town of Tal Afar. Essentially, the idea is that "a large operation is necessary to defeat the terrorist organization . . . a reconstituted police force and the Iraqi army . . . improvement in security . . . on the back end . . . conduct reconstruction, to rekindle hope among the population" (McMaster 2007). Many of the participants have assessed that the experience in Tal Afar "the clear-hold-build model is effective" (Yingling 2006). This view was selected as a case study of success in Secretary of State's briefing to the Senate Foreign Relations Committee in 2007 (Washington Post 2007). In both cases, military leaders on the ground were under pressure to develop new ideas to confront a dynamic environment. This reflects tremendous leadership at the operational and tactical level, but it also illustrates the 2001 version of FM 3-0's inability to serve its function.

These firsthand accounts reflect the complexity of the environment in Iraq with different ethnic and sectarian groups committing violence against each other. Furthermore, the inability of the existing doctrine forced many of the soldiers on the ground to develop new methods to confront a growing insurgency. In short, the evidence shows that there was an identity conflict during this period and the existing military doctrine could not adequately address this complex problem.

Institutional Reflection

Throughout this long and protracted conflict, the U.S. Army has commissioned several official reports to analyze and study the events in Iraq. *On Point, On Point II*, and *In Contact* are just some of the institutional publications, produced by Army's Combat Studies Institute, which tried to capture events in Iraq at the tactical and operational levels. While *On Point* (Fontenot et al. 2004) focuses on the initial period of OIF and *In Contact* (Robertson 2006) covers exclusively at the tactical level operations, *On Point II* (Wright et al. 2008) centers much of its discussions on stabilization and COIN operations from mid-2003 to early 2005, detailing many of the struggles and attempts to solve this complex problem. More specifically, *On Point II* tries to offer an evaluation and critique to the events in Iraq by examining issues such as the applicability of the existing doctrine, the rise of insurgency, and the attempt to conduct a COIN centric operation. The authors of *On Point II* were not afraid to point out some of the key mistakes that directly led to the quagmire in Iraq.

Firstly, *On Point II* offers a direct criticism of the 2001 FM 3-0 and its practicality in guiding the Army through a complex operation such as OIF. It argues that "the Army often fulfilled its role of securing the nation by preparing for . . . conventional wars. In 2001 the Army reinforced this understanding . . . by stating in its capstone doctrinal work, Field Manual (FM) 3-0 . . . when OIF became a full spectrum campaign . . . the U.S. Army found itself in a conflict for which it was less than well prepared" (Wright et al. 2008, 49). This is a scathing review of Army's own doctrine and its ability to prepare the forces for war prior to 2003. Also, this is also a criticism toward Army's actual performance and ability to adapt while in combat. The argument that the Army has been consistent in its emphasis conventional warfare is not without merit. Above all, the lack of stability planning, better known as phase four planning, clearly demonstrates a clear failure of leadership and doctrine as well. In the assessment, *On Point II* discovers that "the CENTCOM staff spent a greater amount of time on the preparation for the staging of forces in Kuwait and initial offensive operations than it did on what might happen after

65

the toppling of the Saddam regime" (Wright et al. 2008, 76). The lack of planning on stability operation foreshadows the eventual fiasco occurred later in which many still believed that it is possible to fight your way out of this problem.

In short, Iraq illustrates that the 2001 FM 3-0, although it proclaims to represents a "Full Spectrum" operation in its thinking, overtly places a stronger emphasis toward offensive and defensive operations. *On Point II* argues that, "without relying on doctrine . . . Army units transitioned to a practice of full spectrum operations that, by the end of 2003, followed many well-established principles of counterinsurgency warfare (Wright et al. 2008, 87). This analysis clearly exposes first the failure, during the initial stage, to follow the existing doctrine in constructing a proper stabilization plan and the inadequacy of the doctrine when it could no longer provide a workable solution to the soldiers on the ground.

In addition to discovering the shortcomings of the existing doctrine, *On Point II* also examines the rise of insurgency and the root causes behind it. Fundamentally, there was a very clear understanding amongst the military planners that "instability and violence were probable after Saddam's fall" (Wright et al. 2008, 89). Furthermore, some assessed that there was a brief window of opportunity to prevent insurgency from happening, but the actual attempt to address the rise insurgency came too late (Wright et al. 2008, 89). At its origin, *On Point II* argues that the origins of Iraq discontent could be traced from the fall of Baghdad and the lawlessness within the city, the De-Baathification, and the disbanding of the Iraqi Army as the most important issues that contributed to the rise of insurgency (Wright et al. 2008, 89-98). This analysis offers a perspective analyzing the Sunni discontent and some experts have assessed that these events provided key ingredients for Sunni insurgency to flourish (Wright et al. 2008, 92).

This discontent did enable many of the Sunni to join various insurgent groups to fight

against "the occupiers." Yet, there is another aspect of insurgency did not receive much

attention.

On Point II's assessment offers an explanation as to the reason why insurgency

was able to grow, but the existing tension amongst various ethnic and sectarian groups

did not receive much attention in this analysis. *On Point II* briefly mentions the concern

within U.S. military that "Saddam's army had been a brutal institution [with a] historical

employment of his army in the repression of Shia and Kurdish populations" (Wright et al.

2008, 95). This is true, but both Shia and Kurds were also planning for their own

arrangements in a more sophisticated way that *On Point II* does not spend much effort to

cover. The only exception is the rise of Muqtada al-Sadr and the Mahdi Army. *On Point

II* views the Mahdi Army as a key insurgent group that has a comparable capability as

other Sunni groups such as former regime loyalists and AQIZ (Wright et al. 2008, 109-

110). Yet, the focus remains on Mahdi Army's attacks against the American forces, with

no discussion on Mahdi Army or other Shia militia groups committing acts of violence

against the Sunni population. In short, the analysis offers a valuable perspective into

insurgency in Iraq, but the analysis fails to understand the rising tension amongst various

ethnic and sectarian groups.

The official institutional reflection, through *On Point II*, illustrates an active

attempt to discover what went wrong and to capture valuable lessons from this period for

the benefit of future generation. This analysis has captured many of the important

elements such as the complexity of insurgency and related support networks (Wright et al. 2008, 103). The analysis echoes many of the practitioners' experience. Despite the fact that *On Point II* did not capture the tension amongst various ethnic and sectarian groups, this analysis does offer a more thorough lessons learned in assisting the Army to better understand the operational environment.

The next iteration of FM 3-0: The 2008 revision

The events in Iraq illustrated that the 2001 version of FM 3-0 could not adequately address many of the challenges facing the U.S. Army. Unable to serve its purpose in a complex environment, the 2001 version of FM 3-0 was not a useful framework to explain the current operational environment to units preparing for their deployments to Iraq. From Kretchik's perspective, many of the units had placed more emphasis on the informal practices than the formal doctrine (Chiarelli and Michaelis 2005; McMaster 2007). As a result, the U.S. Army had to create and write a doctrine that would address this problem in a newly published FM 3-24 *Counterinsurgency*, which became a widely read manual in both Iraq and Afghanistan. Finally, the revised version of FM 3-0 officially published in 2008 provides a more thorough discussion on the contemporary characteristics of warfare.

A manual that filled the gap: FM 3-24

As a solution to resolve the dire situation in Iraq, the publication of FM 3-24, *Counterinsurgency*, became an instrumental doctrine because the U.S. Army had not updated its COIN manual for almost twenty years (US Army 2006, Foreword). In addition, forces in Iraq did not have an officially approved doctrine as a reference to conduct COIN operations because the 2001 version of FM 3-0 was largely an irrelevant and ineffectual doctrine. Although people like McMaster was quite successful in Tal Afar, the "clear, hold, and build" framework was not officially sanctioned and many leaders at the tactical level were very confused about the proper way to conduct COIN operations (Adamczyk 2012, 12). The development of a new COIN manual started before David Petraeus' arrival as the Commander of U.S. Army's Combined Arms Center. The interim COIN manual, FMI 3-07.22, was published on October 2004 (Kaplan 2013, 133-7). However, the revision process and the final publication of FM 3-24 were under Petraeus' direct supervision (Kaplan 2013, chapter 15). Furthermore, FM 3-24 is a joint manual between the U.S. Army and Marines Corps because both services were trying to address the inadequacy of the existing doctrine and the complex problems in Iraq.

FM 3-24 discusses many key issues that the U.S. forces were confronting in Iraq and provides a framework as a potential solution to solve this complex problem. First, the manual addresses the fundamental insurgency and COIN aspects in the initial chapter. In discussing the aspect of insurgency, the manual covers the basic insurgent approaches such as conspiratorial, military-focused, urban, the protracted popular war, identity focused, and coalition (US Army 2006, 1-5). Many of these approaches echo the arguments from Kaldor (2012), Münkler (2004), and Smith (2005). For example, the manual uses the Ma Zedong's theory of protracted war and North Vietnamese Dau Trahn as two historical examples to illustrate the prolonged nature of a counterinsurgency operation (US Army 2006, 1-6). In addition to the discussion on a protracted insurgency, the manual also discusses how insurgent elements would "mobilize support based on the common identity of religious, affiliation, clan, tribe, or ethnic group" (US Army 2006, 1-8). This section fits the fundamental concept of an identity conflict and it echoes Kaldor's emphasis on the importance of identity politics on contemporary warfare (2012, 79-90). In short, FM 3-24 discusses many key features of an identity conflict in describing an insurgency.

In addition to a discussion on Maoist theory, FM 3-24 also covers important elements that are pertinent to conduct a successful COIN operation. For example, the manual discusses the importance of unity of effort among civilian and military activities in chapter 2, intelligence activities in chapter three, designing a COIN campaign in chapter four, execution a COIN campaign in chapter five, and developing host-nation security forces in chapter six (US Army 2006). In short, these chapters are designed to provide military practitioners a basic but important framework as a reference in conducting a complex COIN operation.

Since its publication, some have called FM 3-24 as a "transformational manual [that] represents a conscious effort to reshape the way the Army and Marine Corps think about warfare" (Linn 2007, 81). However, the manual is not without critique from those who think that "this new army doctrinal manual presented a simplistic set of actions to counter an insurgency that distorted what [some] had witness in 2006 . . . the section in the beginning . . . was a jumble of dreamy statements" (Gentile 2013, xvi). Despite some vociferous critiques from people such as Gian Gentile, an Army officer with experience in Iraq and later taught history at West Point, many have assessed that the manual's impact is "demonstrable" (Cohen 2010, 90) and a significant effort to reframe "a new American way of war" (Kaplan 2013). Thus, it is evidently clear that FM 3-24 is a doctrine that has trumped the importance of actual capstone manual, the 2001 FM 3-0, and its ability to relate and frame the actual operational environment to the soldiers on the frontline.

A Revised Manual: The 2008 FM 3-0

The revised FM 3-0, officially published in 2008, has captured many of the important lessons learned in the recent conflicts. From Army's perspective, this manual proclaims to "present the fundamental principles and concepts that guide the direction of Army operations rather than a checklist for success" (Wallace 2008, 2). Moreover, the updated manual has developed a more progressive approach as far as its outlook. For example, the latest version includes such phrases as "war among people," as a way to describe the contemporary operational environment. On the other hand, the 2008 FM 3-0 continues to develop the "Full Spectrum" concept and focus on "Unified Action." In short, the 2008 FM 3-0 is a manual that tries to adapt to the environment during a contentious period when Army forces were facing direct combat operations on daily basis without a proper manual that offers a reasonable explanation as to how they should fight and win.

One of the key elements in the new FM 3-0 is the setting context of the operational environment through adding the operational variables, PMESII-PT. PMESII-PT stands for political, military, economic, social, infrastructure, information, physical environment, and time. The Army has chosen to incorporate key elements from the joint doctrine and PMESII-PT is one of the new items added to the doctrine. Operational variables are instrumental in facilitating and assisting the military to understand the environment on the ground. After all, each geographic location has a different dynamic and "operational variables describe not only the military aspects of an operational environment but also the population's influence on it" (US Army 2008, 1-5). Together

with the mission variables, METT-TC, the purpose of PMESII-PT is to assist "Army

forces . . . to understand and analyze the broad environment in which they are conducting

operations [and] to focus on analysis on specific elements of the environment that apply

to their mission" (US Army 2008, 1-5). In short, the decision to incorporate the joint

concept into the latest Army manual reflects the continual emphasis to create a coherent

manual. Furthermore, PMESII-PT is a useful tool to analyze and describe the operational

environment, which would also facilitate the tactical and operational commander to have

a better situational awareness.

In addition to a newly defined operational environment, another modification in

FM 3-0 is the discussion on the spectrum of conflict and operational themes. These

concepts facilitate the learning and understanding of an operational environment by

providing a framework and tool to "understand and visualize the level of violence and

corresponding role of the military in resolving a conflict" (US Army 2008, 2-1). This is a

clear recognition that the level of violence in any conflict can either ascend or descend

and it is critical to seek and establish a firm understanding of the situation and issues on

the ground, using operational and mission variables.

As a part of the spectrum of conflict, operational themes are designed to

accompany this framework. The creation of operation theme "describes the character of

the dominant major operation being conducted at any time within a land force

commander's area of operations . . . helps to convey the nature of the major operation to

the force to facilitate common understanding" (US Army 2008, 2-3). These operation

themes include peacetime military engagement, limited intervention, peace operations, irregular warfare, and major combat operations. It is an attempt to relook the previously established full spectrum concept in the 2001 FM 3-0. The purpose is to "describe the major operation's general characteristics" (US Army 2008, 2-5). This framework enables a more fluid and seamless transition in describing a conflict, unlike the previous FM 3-0 in which one can only choose either war or MOOTW as a way to characterize a military operation.

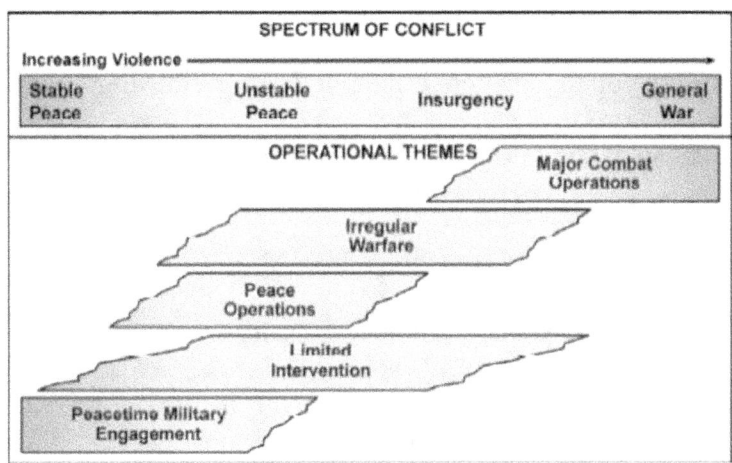

Figure 3.   The Spectrum of Conflict and Operational Themes

Source: Department of the Army, Field Manual (FM) 3-0, *Operations* (Washington, DC: Government Printing Office, 2008), 2-5.

The new manual continues its theme of full spectrum operation, but it is now a part of Army's operational concept which defined as "combine offensive, defensive, and stability or civil support operations simultaneously as part of an interdependent joint force . . . to create opportunities to achieve decisive results" (US Army 2008, 3-1). It is important to highlight the effort to see stability operations as "coequal with offensive and defensive operations" (US Army 2008, D-3). This is a direct response to the events in Afghanistan and Iraq where military forces learned the importance of a failed stability operation can do to the success of a military campaign. From the attempt to elevate the importance of stability operation, the 2008 FM 3-0 also describes that "an inherent, complimentary relationship exists between using lethal force and applying military capabilities for nonlethal purposes" (US Army 2008, 3-4). This echoes with the understanding that military strength and technological superiority will not be sufficient to solve a complex problem. Thus, a more thorough and comprehensive solution is required to confront a challenging operational environment. In short, this thinking reflects a deeper understanding and appreciation of the contemporary operational environment.

Does the 2008 version recognize Identity Conflict as a cause?

As a revision, the 2008 version of FM 3-0 has incorporated many of the shortcomings from its previous edition through many of the hard-learned lessons in combat. Many valuable lessons learned and new ideas have been incorporated to the new doctrine and the 2008 version of FM 3-0 has come a long way to be much closer in recognizing identity conflict as an important feature in contemporary conflict. Yet, there are areas in the 2008 version of FM 3-0 could not adequately answer without drastically altering the purpose of a military doctrine. After all, the literature review section has already discussed the purpose of doctrine and that purpose is not about presenting a scholarly argument or generating a new debate. Nonetheless, the 2008 version of FM 3-0 has managed to cover many of important features of the "New Wars" theory in that it has come a long way from its previous editions with a more nuance explanation on the diverse and complicated nature of the operational environment. In short, the Army has recognized the presence of identity conflict without actually stating it in words.

First, the 2008 version of FM 3-0 has discussed some characteristics of the "New Wars" theory in a limited way. Firstly, there is a strong recognition in the non-state actors and their involvement in the conflict. Yet, Kaldor's analysis is more than just the participation of non-state actors because the use of identity politics is a key element for these non-state actors to exploit the fragmentation amongst different groups (Kaldor 2012, 7-8). The manual does mention non-state actors as an important player, but it does not provide a coherent argument. For example, the manual lists a few trends such as globalization, technology, and resource demand to describe areas that will influence ground forces operations, but there is no mention of people exploiting ethnic or religious difference (US Army 2008, 1-1). Secondly, the FM 3-0 does identify the complexity of threat and its ability to employ creative means to finance and support a conflict (US Army 2008, 1-5). Thus, this portion coincides with the "New Wars" theory's argument on globalized war economy as a new method to finance a conflict. In short, the 2008 version of FM 3-0 contains some elements of the "New Wars" theory in its content, but these two works are not necessary compatible with each other. Thus, one cannot say that Kaldor's ideas (2012) truly reflect in the 2008 version of FM 3-0.

As a term, the era of persistent conflict reflects Münkler's argument (2004) on the protracted nature of an identity conflict. During his tenure as Army's Chief of Staff, General William Casey argues that concept of "the era of persistent conflict" (Casey 2007) and the phrase became embedded within the 2008 version of FM 3-0. The concept of persistent conflict coincides with the argument that identity conflict is really a multigeneration and prolonged struggle. One cannot simply expect any short military operation would be sufficient to resolve a long conflict with ancient historical roots. The doctrine clearly address this aspect by stating that "our nation will continue to be engaged in an era of persistent conflict–a period of protracted confrontation among states, non-state, and individual actors increasingly willing to use violence to achieve their political and ideological ends" (US Army 2008, Foreword). In short, the 2008 version of FM 3-0 has partially acknowledged the enduring nature of identity conflict in describing the era of persistent conflict.

Lastly, the 2008 version of FM 3-0 recognizes a key feature of identity conflict as it partly recognizes Smith's "War Amongst the People" argument (2005). In the opening foreword, the 2008 version of FM 3-0 states that, "this persistent conflict . . . will be complex, multidimensional, and increasingly fought among the people" (US Army 2008, Foreword). This is a direct link from Smith's thesis (2005) to the actual FM 3-0 text. However, one has to look very closely in the actual text to see there is a difference between them. In Smith's "War Amongst the People," there are six characteristics (2005, 19). The literature review chapter has examined these elements and it is obvious that the phrase amongst the people, according to Smith, means more than just conducting operations in an urban environment. On the other hand, the 2008 version of FM 3-0 characterizes "war among the people" as "a battle of wills–a contest for dominance over people" (US Army 2008, 1-5). The depiction of conducting military operations among urban population coincides with just one out of six characteristics in Smith's thesis (2005, 19). Moreover, this is just another attempt to reiterate the previous emphasis on the urbanization trend in the world and the likelihood of conduct military operation in such environment. The 2008 version of FM 3-0 does not truly reflect Smith's core argument that "the people in the streets and houses and fields . . . are the battlefield . . . civilians are the targets, objectives to be won, as much as an opposing force" (Smith 2005, 6). The concept of "War Amongst the People" is a nuance argument on the diverse nature of the current operational environment. This is an aspect that the 2008 version of FM 3-0 did not accurately capture in its emphasis on "war among the people," which is a regurgitation of the previous Army concept on urban operations. As a result, the 2008 FM 3-0 did not fully capture the essence of the "New Wars" theory in its text and one cannot rightfully argue that Smith's "War Amongst the People" (2005) is included in the updated capstone manual.

In all, the 2008 FM 3-0 has partially recognized identity conflict as a character of contemporary warfare that should be considered in military planning and execution. Without actually stating it in the doctrine, the 2008 FM 3-0 has covered many of the features in its writing that it is easy to identity key features of the "New Wars" theory embedded within the text.

<u>Summary</u>

From 2001 to 2008, the U.S. Army has conducted other military operations around the world such as Operation Enduring Freedom in Afghanistan. Yet, Iraq dominated most of the attention during this period. From a successful offensive operation in the beginning, OIF has turned into a "long, hard slog" (Rumsfeld quote in Roberts 2003) when the U.S. military could not adequately address Iraq's post-conflict environment, which descend into chaos. Within this complex and post-conflict environment, one has to acknowledge that historical forces did play a critical role. The fragile and unstable environment aggravated an old and persistent animosity amongst the Sunni, Shia, and the Kurds. The inability to confront a rising insurgency led to an outburst of sectarian violence throughout Iraq.

Amid this protracted conflict with a long historical root, operational experience in Iraq also illustrates the multifaceted aspect of post-Saddam Iraq. Unfortunately, the U.S. had chosen to see any attack in Iraq as merely perpetrated by "Anti-Iraqi Forces," a simplistic and duplicitous way of describing a complex environment in a naive and ignorant fashion. Firsthand accounts and official studies have clearly illustrated that the situation on the ground was far more intricate than many realized. These reflections have portrayed the events in a different form than the official announcement about the actual progress in Iraq.

Unable to use the existing doctrine to cope with a rising insurgency, many units have chosen to adopt what Kretchik (2011) called "informal practice" to confront a deadly enemy. Some had successes while many failed. The publication of FM 3-24 ushered a new era for the struggle in Iraq. This manual became a more useful tool than the Army's capstone doctrine, which was in a state of despair for its inability to address the operational environment in Iraq. Yet, the revised FM 3-0 has managed to capture many of the key lessons learned in Iraq and document these aspects into a coherent form as a way to shape and inform how Army should think about contemporary warfare and conflict.

Finally, the identity conflict thesis, using the "New Wars" theory as its foundation, has become more visible in the updated version of FM 3-0. The 2008 version of FM 3-0 has discussed some key features of the "New Wars" theory in its text. From

Mary Kaldor (2012), Herfried Münkler (2004), to Rupert Smith (2005), these scholars and their writings have become an important part in helping the Army to better understand and confront a dynamic and changing environment with many old and historical issues and grievances deeply entrenched within a globalized world. In short, the doctrine has accepted many of the key arguments from these authors and many of the hard and painful lessons learned from bloody and costly conflict in places such as Iraq.

By 2008, the U.S. Army has partially recognized that identity conflict is an important feature in the contemporary operational environment. Through the updated FM 3-0, the doctrine has incorporated many of the essential elements of the "New Wars" theory. By recognition these features, the Army has accepted the fact that the operational environment is far more complex and requires a persistent effort to address many of the tough issues around the world. In short, the nature of an identity conflict represents an enduring struggle amongst different racial, ethnic, religious, and sectarian groups that has a deep historical root. No one can truly resolve these conflicts through simplistic thinking and monolithic approach. The U.S. Army has come a long way from a conventional focused version of FM 100-5 in 1993 to a more subtle and balanced version of FM 3-0 in 2008.

CHAPTER 6

CONCLUSIONS AND RECOMMENDATIONS

> History is, in its essentials, the science of change. It knows and it teaches that it is impossible to find two events that are ever exactly alike, because the conditions from which they spring are never identical . . . the lesson it teaches is not that what happened yesterday will necessarily happen tomorrow, or that the past will go on reproducing itself. By examining how and why yesterday differed from the day before, it can reach conclusions which will enable it to foresee how tomorrow will differ from yesterday.
>
> — Marc Bloch, *Strange Defeat*

Introduction

The purpose of this thesis is to examine whether the U.S. Army has accepted the identity conflict thesis as a key characteristic in framing the current operational environment. This chapter provides a summary of key points based on the overall research finding. Furthermore, a list of recommendations will accompany the conclusions as a way to provide a meaningful tool to broaden the spectrum of understanding. Lastly, this chapter recommends some areas for future research based on this research's analysis.

Conclusions

This study has utilized two case studies to examine the primary research question. Through a systematic approach, this research has discovered that the U.S. Army has not fully accepted the identity conflict argument as a framework to understand the contemporary operational environment. Doctrinally, the U.S. Army began the post-Cold War era with an updated capstone manual, the 1993 version of FM 100-5, and this manual was incapable of providing a useful framework for American soldiers to understand the operational environment in Bosnia. Army's operational experience in

Bosnia has illustrated how different groups could exploit ethnic or religious tension for their own political gains. Yet, the primary lesson coming out of the Balkan experience focuses on Army's inability to deploy more rapidly to support a peacekeeping operation. Although some changes were made based on the Balkan experience, the new capstone manual, the 2001 version of FM 3-0, continues to reside its philosophical thinking primarily within the traditional concept on warfare. This has proven to be a problematic presumption for the U.S. Army in preparing for the next major conflict.

The episode in Iraq further illustrates Army's inability to apply the lessons learned from combat into its capstone doctrine. After the end of major combat operation, various mistakes led to the rise of insurgency in Iraq. Complicated by the fact that the Bush Administration refused to recognize the existence of an insurgency, the U.S. Army did not have a useful framework to assist its soldiers to conceptualize this complex dynamic in Iraq. Although there were some military practitioners who creatively applied various "informal practices" to confront a rising insurgency, the U.S. Army did not have a comprehensive approach to meet this challenge until the publication of FM 3-24 and General David Petraeus assuming the role as the overall commander in Iraq. Later, the 2008 version of FM 3-0 illustrates some progressive ideas in its approach, but the overall tone remains within the traditional way of thinking. In all, the 2008 version of FM 3-0 has some elements that resonate with the identity conflict thesis, but this does not represent a complete acceptance in recognizing the identity conflict thesis as an important characteristic of contemporary warfare and operational environment.

In all, Army's experience in the post-Cold War era has illustrated a history of repeated failures to apply the lessons learned from its recent past. Often, these lessons came at a heavy human price. Yet, the U.S. Army has chosen to maintain its thinking within the traditional way of warfare, an approach that has shown its inability to conceptualize the contemporary operational environment. Perhaps the U.S. Army should seriously consider whether the traditional way of warfare is still a viable approach to confront an uncertain future.

Recommendations

Through this research project, there are several recommendations that are valuable in shaping Army's understanding in the contemporary operational environment and future doctrinal development. These recommendations are by no means a panacea to the current problem but a list of ideas that one should consider as a part of generating a livelier and robust discussion that would be beneficial in enriching the forces with a more thorough knowledge on the current operational environment.

As a reflection on the development of both 2001 and 2008 version of FM 3-0, both manuals claim to be revolutionary in nature, but the reality does not show a truly radical and groundbreaking doctrine. Perhaps, both manuals are more evolutionary than revolutionary. To be a revolutionary change, one has to embrace a different philosophical approach in its thinking. Much of the current doctrinal philosophy originates either from Antonio Jomini or from Carl von Clausewitz (Kretchik 2011). There seems to be a disinclination within the Army to consider other ideas outside of these two military thinkers who wrote their seminal works in the nineteenth century by framing their ideas based on the Napoleonic era. Kaldor (2012), Münkler (2004), and Smith (2005) present a different argument that challenges how one should view the contemporary operational environment. These authors represent a wave of new ideas that should bring some fresh thinking into a seemingly static and stagnant institutional culture.

Beyond Kaldor (2012), Münkler (2004), and Smith (2005), one can also apply a more radical approach in developing a different perspective. In dissecting the dichotomy between problem-solving and critical theory, Robert Cox has argued that "problem-solving theory takes the world as it finds it, with the prevailing social and power relationship and institutions into which they are organized [and] critical theory . . . stands apart from the prevailing order of the world and asks how that order came about" (1981, 128-9). Perhaps critical theory can be a tool to better examine and analyze whether the existing institutional approach is adequate and whether a different method is needed to generate a better solution.

On a more practical recommendation, the ability to gather lessons learned and incorporate those lessons into the doctrinal development in a more responsive manner is a necessity for the future. The Bosnian case study shows that many institutional studies on Army's experience were completed after the publication of 2001 version FM 3-0. Although many military practitioners have firsthand experience in the Balkans, the majority of Army forces did not have the benefit of a Balkan deployment to learn some of the key lessons. The episode in Iraq reflects a more rapid institutional reflection and it has to do with the severity of the situation on the ground that triggered a sense of urgency. In sum, a capstone manual has to consider the recent operational experience, across all spectrums, as an important reference point. To do so, it would enable the doctrinal development to reach a better and more judicious analysis.

These recommendations are not prescriptive. Rather, these are just ideas that would enable others to generate additional thoughts and creative solutions in the development of the next capstone manual.

Areas for Future Research

This research project has a recommendation for some research areas that others can examine and analyze. First, Army's Doctrine 2015 concept is a good area to examine whether the U.S. Army has accepted the identity conflict thesis in its latest doctrinal publication. Doctrine 2015 (see for example US Army 2011; US Army 2012; US Army 2014) reflects Army's latest operational thinking and ideas on future warfare. Doctrine 2015 has set out to provide a more dynamic and innovative approach in the post-Afghanistan and Iraq operational environment. With the evolving crises happening in places such as Syria, Libya, Ukraine, Iraq, Sub-Saharan Africa, and Afghanistan, one can apply whether the identity conflict thesis is an applicable criterion to evaluate Doctrine 2015.

Another future research idea is using a different theoretical framework. For example, Stathis Kalyvas has made an argument that, "civil wars are not binary conflicts but complex and ambiguous processes that foster an apparently massive, through variable, mix of identities and actions" (2003, 475). Instead of examining various identity divides, this is an attempt to peel off the outer layer of an armed conflict and looks more closely at the issues on the ground, at the local level. More specifically, Kalyvas argues that local issues can be a driving factor for violence and local actors often take advantage of conflict to settle private conflicts (2003, 475-6).

In *The Logics of Violence in Civil War*, Kalyvas has put together a coherent, comprehensive and persuasive argument in analyzing and separating the difference between civil war violence and the logic of violence in civil war (2006). From a positivist approach, Kalyvas devotes a much greater depth in explaining the intricacy and convolutedness of violence in civil wars. Moreover, Kalyvas challenges many of the existing theories (see for example Collier and Hoeffler 1998) that focus "exclusively [at] macrolevel motivations and dynamics" (2006, 6). From his perspective, Kalyvas has placed an emphasis on local cleavages as an important reference in understanding violence. It seems that one cannot truly understand violence at the local level without knowing issues at that level as well. In short, Kalyvas (2006) has provided an interesting and valuable perspective that offers another way of looking at the current operational environment.

Summary

This research project has examined whether the U.S. Army has accepted the identity conflict thesis as a part of Army's capstone manual in describing the contemporary operational environment. Through case studies from Bosnia and Iraq, there are many useful lessons to be learned and applied in the future doctrinal development. At the same time, one has to be aware of how each case study is unique and one should not automatically apply one case to another without a proper understanding. In the end, it is all about finding the best way to prepare the Army for tomorrow's challenge, ensuring that we are accountable to both the nation we serve and the soldiers we lead.

REFERENCE LIST

1-41 Infantry (IN). 1997. "Bosnia AAR." Fort Riley, KS: First Infantry Division Museum Archive.

Adamczyk, Matthew. 2012. Interviewed by Jenna Fike. January 3. Combat Studies Institute Operational Leadership Experiences. Accessed July 10, 2014. http://cgsc.contentdm.oclc.org/cdm/landingpage/collection/p4013coll13.

Ancker, Clinton, and Mike Scully. 2010. "Army Doctrine Publication 3-0: An Opportunity to Meet the Challenges of the Future." *Military Review* 43, no. 1: 38-42.

Baumann, Robert, George Gawrych, and Walter Kretchik. 2004. *Armed Peacekeeping in Bosnia.* Fort Leavenworth, KS: Combat Studies Institute Press.

Belcher, Eric. 2012. Interviewed by Jenna Fike. April 23. Combat Studies Institute Operational Leadership Experiences. Accessed July 10, 2014. http://cgsc.contentdm.oclc.org/cdm/landingpage/collection/p4013coll13.

Berdal, Mats R. 2003. "How New Are New Wars? Global Economic Change and the Study of Civil War." *Global Governance* 9, no. 4: 477-502.

Birtle, Andrew. 1998. *U.S. Army Counterinsurgency and Contingency Operations Doctrine: 1860-1941.* Washington, DC: Center of Military History Press.

————. 2006. *U.S. Army Counterinsurgency and Contingency Operations Doctrine: 1942-1976.* Washington, DC: Center of Military History Press.

Bloch, Marc. 1946. *Strange Defeat: A Statement of Evidence Written in 1940.* London: W. W. Norton.

British Broadcasting Company (BBC). 2006. *Iraqi Blast Damages Shia Shrine.* 22 February. Accessed September 1, 2014. http://news.bbc.co.uk/2/hi /middle_east/4738472.stm.

Buzan, Barry, and Lene Hansen. 2009. *The Evolution of International Security Studies.* Cambridge: Cambridge University Press.

Casey, George. 2007. "Persistent Conflict: The New Strategic Environment." Address given to the Los Angeles World Affairs Council, September 27, 2007.

Chandrasekaran, Rajiv. 2006. *Imperial Life in the Emerald City: Inside Iraq's Green Zone.* New York: Knopf.

Chiarelli, Peter, and Patrick Michaelis. 2005. "Winning the Peace: The Requirement for Full-Spectrum Operations." *Military Review* 85, no. 4: 4-17.

Clausewitz, Carl Von. 1976. *On War*. Edited and translated by Michael Howard and Peter Paret. Princeton: Princeton University Press,

Clinton, Hilary. 2011. "America's Pacific Century." *Foreign Policy,* no.189: 56-63.

Cohen, Raphael. 2010. "A Tale of Two Manuals." *Prism* 2, no. 1: 87-100.

Collier, Paul, and Anke Hoeffler. 1998. "On Economic Causes of Civil War." *Oxford Economic Paper 50*: 563-573.

———. 2004. "Greed and Grievance in Civil War." *Oxford Economic Paper 56:* 563-595.

Cordesman, Anthony. 2006. *Iraq's Sectarian and Ethnic Violence and the Evolving Insurgency: Development through mid-December 2006.* Washington, DC: Center for Strategic and International Studies. Accessed October 10, 2014. http://www.comw.org/warreport/fulltext/061214cordesman.pdf.

Cox, Robert. 1981. "Social Forces, States and World Orders: Beyond International Relations Theory." *Millennium* 10, no. 2: 126-155.

Dasse, Christopher. 2007. "Clausewitz and Small Wars." In *Clausewitz in the Twenty-First Century*, edited by Hew Strachan and Andreas Herberg-Rothe, 182-195. Oxford: Oxford University Press.

Dempsey, Jason. 2007. Interviewed by Laurence Lessard. January 31. Combat Studies Institute Operational Leadership Experiences. Accessed July 10, 2014. http://cgsc.contentdm.oclc.org/cdm/landingpage/collection/p4013coll13.

Dempsey, Martin. 2014. "Remarks at the National Defense University." Accessed August 10, 2014. http://www.jcs.mil/DesktopModules/DigArticle/Print.aspx?PortalId =36&ModuleId=8258&Article=7819.

Echevarria, Antulio. 2005. "Deconstructing the Theory of Fourth-Generation War." *Contemporary Security Policy* 26, no. 2: 233-241.

———. 2007. *Clausewitz and Contemporary War.* Oxford: Oxford University Press.

English, Richard. 2013. *Modern War: A Very Short Introduction,* Oxford: Oxford University Press.

Fearon, James. 2005. "Primary Commodity Exports and Civil War." *Journal of Conflict Resolution* 49, no. 4: 483-507.

Filkins, Dexter. 2008. *The Forever War.* New York: Knopf.

Fukuyama, Francis. 1992. *The End of History and the Last Man.* New York: The Free Press.

Gentile, Gian. 2013. *Wrong Turn: America's Deadly Embrace of Counterinsurgency.* New York: New Press.

Gray, Colin. 2010. "War–Continuity in Change, and Change in Continuity." *Parameters* (Summer): 5-13.

Gordon, Michael, and Bernard Trainor. 2006. *Cobra II: The Inside Story of the Invasion and Occupation of Iraq.* New York: Pantheon.

———. 2012. *The Endgame: The Inside Story of the Struggle for Iraq, from George W. Bush to Barack Obama.* New York: Vintage.

Hammes, Thomas. 2006. *The Sling and The Stone: On War in the 21st Century.* St Paul: Zenith Press.

Heuser, Beatrice. 2007. "Clausewitz's Ideas of Strategy and Victory." In *Clausewitz in the Twenty-First Century*, edited by Hew Strachan and Andreas Herberg-Rothe, 138-162. Oxford: Oxford University Press.

Hoffman, Frank. 2007. *Conflict in the 21st Century: The Rise of Hybrid Wars.* Arlington: Potomac Institute for Policy Studies.

Holsti, Kalevi. 1996. *The State, War and the State of War.* Cambridge: Cambridge University Press.

Howard, Michael. 2002. *Clausewitz: A Very Short Introduction.* Oxford: Oxford University Press.

Huntington, Samuel. 1993. "Clash of Civilization." *Foreign Affairs* 72, no. 3: 22-49.

Jackson, Aaron. 2013. *The Root of Military Doctrine: Change and Continuity in Understanding the Practice of Warfare.* Fort Leavenworth, KS: Combat Studies Institutes Press.

Kaldor, Mary. 2012. *New and Old Wars: Organized Violence in a Global Era.* 3rd ed. London: Polity.

Kalyvas, Stathis. 2001. "New and Old Civil Wars: A Valid Distinction?" *World Politics* 54, no. 1: 99-118.

———. 2006. *The Logic of Violence in Civil War.* New York: Cambridge University Press.

Kaplan, Fred. 2013. *The Insurgents: David Petraeus and the Plot to Change the American Way of War.* New York: Simon and Shuster.

Kaplan, Robert. 2003. *Balkan Ghosts: A Journal Through History.* New York: St. Martin's Press.

———. 2000. "The Coming Anarchy." *World Policy Journal* 17, no. 2: 95-96.

Keen, David. 1998. *Adelphi Paper 320, The Economic Functions of Violence in Civil Wars.* Oxford: Oxford University Press.

Kuhn, Thomas. 1962. *The Structure of Scientific Revolutions.* New York: University of Chicago Press.

Lake, David, and Donald Rothchild. 1996. "Containing Fear: The Origin and Management of Ethnic Conflict." *International Security* 21, no. 2: 41-75.

Layne, Christopher. 1993. "The Unipolar Illusion: Why New great Powers Will Rise." *International Security* 17, no. 4: 5-51.

Le Billion, Philippe. 2012. *Wars of Plunder: Conflicts, Profits and the Politics of Resources.* London: Hurst.

Lewis, Bernard. 1997. *The Middle East: A Brief History of the Last 2,000 Years.* New York: Scribner.

Linn, Brian. 2007. "Book Review: Doctrine and Vision for Today and the Future." *Army,* November: 80-81.

MacFarland, Sean. 2008. Interviewed by Steven Clay. January 17. Combat Studies Institute Operational Leadership Experiences. Accessed July 10, 2014. http://cgsc.contentdm.oclc.org/cdm/landingpage/collection/p4013coll13.

Mackinlay, John. 1999. "What is new about new wars?" *The RUSI Journal* 144, no. 4: 84-86.

Malešević, Siniša. 2006. *Identity as Ideology: Understanding Ethnicity and Nationalism.* New York: Palgrave Macmillan.

Mansfield, Peter. 1991. *A History of the Middle East.* London: Penguin Books.

McMaster, H. R. 2005. Interview with PBS. Accessed September 10, 2014. http://www.pbs.org/wgbh/pages/frontline/insurgency/interviews/mcmaster.html.

———. 2007. Interview with PBS. Accessed September 10, 2014. http://www.pbs.org/wgbh/pages/frontline/endgame/interviews/mcmaster.html.

Metz, Steven, and Phillip Cuccia. 2011. *Defining War for the 21st Century: 2010 SSI Annual Strategy Conference Report.* Carlisle: Strategic Studies Institute.

Münkler, Herfried. 2004. *The New Wars.* Cambridge: Polity.

Nasr, Vali. 2006. *The Shia Revival: How Conflicts within Islam Will Shape the Future.* New York: Norton.

Newman, Edward. 2004. "The New Wars Debate: A Historical Perspective Is Needed." *Security Dialogue* 35, no. 2: 173-189.

Obama, Barack. 2014. *Commencement Address to the United States Military Academy, West Point.* West Point, New York.

Odierno, Raymond. 2012. "The U.S. Army in a Time of Transition." *Foreign Affairs* 91, no. 3: 7-11.

Oxford English Dictionary (OED). 1989. "War, Conflict, and Identity" Accessed October 1, 2014. http://www.oed.com/.

Packer, George. 2006. *The Assassins' Gate: America in Iraq.* New York: Farrar.

Paparone, Christopher. 2008. "FM 3-0: Operations on the Cusp of Postpositivism" *Small Wars Journal.* Accessed October 1, 2014. http://smallwarsjournal.com/jrnl/art/fm-3-0-operations-on-the-cusp-of-postpositivism

Petraeus, David. 2006. Interviewed by Steven Clay. December 11. Combat Studies Institute Operational Leadership Experiences. Accessed July 10, 2014. http://cgsc.contentdm.oclc.org/cdm/landingpage/collection/p4013coll13.

Popper, Karl. 1959. *The Logic of Scientific Discovery.* New York: Routledge.

Posen, Barry. 1993. "The Security Dilemma and Ethnic Conflict." *Survival* 35, no. 1: 27-47.

Rangelov, Lavor, and Mary Kaldor. 2012. "Persistent Conflict." *Conflict, Security and Development* 12, no. 3: 193-199.

Rick, Thomas, 2006. *Fiasco: The American Military Adventure in Iraq.* New York: Penguin Press.

———. 2009. *The Gamble: General David Petraeus and the American Military Adventure in Iraq, 2006-2008.* New York: Penguin Press.

Roberts, Joel. 2003. "Rummy: Long, Hard Slog in Iraq." *CBS News.* October 23. Accessed October 1, 2014. http://www.cbsnews.com/news/rummy-long-hard-slog-in-iraq/.

Robertson, William, ed. 2006. *In Contact! Case Studies from the Long War: Volume I.* Fort Leavenworth, KS: Combat Studies Institute Press.

Ross, Michael. 2004. "What Do We Know about Natural Resources and Civil War?" *Journal of Peace Research* 41, no. 3: 337-356.

Schuurman, Bart. 2010. "Clausewitz and the New Wars Scholars." *Parameter* 40, no. 1: 89-100.

Simpson, Emile. 2012. *War from the Ground Up.* London: Hurst.

Smith, Rupert. 2005. *The Utility of Force: the Art of War in the Modern War.* New York: Knopf.

Snyder, Jack. 2004. "One World, Rival Theories." *Foreign Policy,* no. 145: 52-62.

Steele, Dennis. 2001. "The Army Launches An Attack-Focused Doctrine For the Joint Fight." *Army Magazine,* August 2001, 41-42.

Strachan, Hew. 2007. "Clausewitz and the Dialectic of War." In *Clausewitz in the Twenty-First Century*, edited by Hew Strachan and Andreas Herberg-Rothe, 1-13. Oxford: Oxford University Press.

———. 2008. "Strategy and the Limitation of War." *Survival* 50, no. 1: 31-54.

———. 2011. "Clausewitz and the First World War." *Journal of Military History,* no. 75: 367-391.

United Kingdom Army (UK Army). 2011. *Army Doctrine Primer*. Swindon: Ministry of Defence.

U.S Department of the Army (US Army). 1993. FM 100-5, *Operations*. Washington, DC: Headquarters, Department of the Army

———. 1997. FM 100-5, *Operations*. Washington, DC: Headquarters, Department of the Army

———. 1998. FM 100-5, *Operations*. Washington, DC: Headquarters, Department of the Army

———. 2001. FM 3-0, *Operations*. Washington, DC: Headquarters, Department of the Army.

———. 2006. FM 3-24, *Counterinsurgency*. Washington, DC: Headquarters, Department of the Army.

———. 2008. FM 3-0, *Operations*. Washington, DC: Headquarters, Department of the Army.

———. 2011. Army Doctrine Publication (ADP) 3-0, *Unified Land Operations*. Washington, DC: Headquarters, Department of the Army.

———. 2012. ADP 3-07, *Stability*. Washington, DC: Headquarters, Department of the Army.

———. 2014. ADP 1-01, *Doctrine Primer*. Washington, DC: Headquarters, Department of the Army.

U.S. Department of Defense (DOD). 2010. *Quadrennial Defense Review*. Washington, DC: Department of Defense.

———. 2012. *Sustaining U.S. Global Leadership: Priorities for 21st Century Defense*. Washington, DC: Department of Defense.

———. 2014. *Quadrennial Defense Review*. Washington, DC: Department of Defense.

Van Creveld, Martin. 1991. *The Transformation of War*. New York: The Free Press.

Wallace, William. 2008. "FM 3-0 Operations: The Army's Blueprint." *Military Review* 88, no. 2: 2-7.

Wallensteen, Peter. 2002. *Understanding Conflict Resolution: War, Peace and the Global System*. London: Sage Publication.

Wass de Czege, Huba, and Antulio Echevarria. 2000. "Insights into a Power Projection Army." *Military Review* 80, no. 3: 3-11.

Washington Post. 2007 "Senate Foreign Relations Committee on President's Iraq Strategy" 11 January. Accessed September 10, 2014. http://www.washingtonpost.com/wp-dyn/content/article/2007/01/11/AR2007011100735.html

West, Bing. *The Strongest Tribe: War, Politics, and the Endgame in Iraq*. New York: Random House.

White House. 2010. *National Security Strategy*. Washington, DC: White House.

Woodard, Bob. 2006. *State of Denial: Bush at War, Part III*. New York: Simon and Schuster.

———. 2008. *The War Within: A Secret White House History, 2006-2008*. New York: Simon and Schuster.

Yingling, Paul. 2006. Interviewed by John McCool. September 22. Combat Studies Institute Operational Leadership Experiences. Accessed July 10, 2014. http://cgsc.contentdm.oclc.org/cdm/landingpage/collection/p4013coll13.